Finding God
in the Evening News

Finding God
in the Evening News

*A Broadcast Journalist
Looks beyond the Headlines*

Jody Dean

Revell
Grand Rapids, Michigan

Published by Fleming H. Revell
a division of Baker Publishing Group
P.O. Box 6287, Grand Rapids, MI 49516-6287
www.revellbooks.com

Printed in the United States of America

Library of Congress Cataloging-in-Publication Data
Dean, Jody, 1949–
    Finding God in the evening news : a broadcast journalist looks beyond the headlines / Jody Dean.
        p.   cm.
    ISBN 0-8007-5972-9 (pbk.)
    1. Christian life. 2. Providence and government of God. 3. Dean, Jody, 1949– 4. Broadcast journalism—United States. I. Title.
BV4509.5.D43 2004
248'.0973—dc22   2004012934

Published in association with the literary agency of The B & B Media Group, Inc., dba The Barnabas Agency, 109 S. Main, Corsicana, TX 75110, www.tbbmedia.com

To Bob and Verna Berry, for their clear picture of Jesus. To my parents, for their hearts and lives. To my children, for their unconditional and undeserved love. To God, for his unrelenting pursuit and blessings. With gratitude and love for which there are no words.

And to Emily. "All these things."

Contents

Contents

Preface

"There's just too much sadness in the world."

"The news is too depressing."

"Where was God when this happened?"

So many people find themselves saying these words. Maybe you've said them. I have.

Despair and discouragement are as close as the next newscast. Many people are almost afraid to open their morning paper for fear of what the headlines will bring. People hurt each other. Lives are lost or ruined. Celebrities and leaders fail and fall. Never mind the problems and disappointments within our own lives and families. A quick glance at the news is all it takes to make us pull down the blinds, call in sick, and cover our heads with a pillow.

Those who do *not* believe in God seem almost *lucky*: They have no need to reconcile the destruction they see all around them with the idea of a loving Creator. But what about those of us who believe in God? Even as we go to church, sing our songs, and pray our prayers, the fear that God is not in control and that all is lost sneaks into our minds. Although we tune to the "right" radio stations, turn away from all those cable news shows, tune out when things get too rough, and try to avoid the heartache altogether, the evidence confronts us daily. We stick our heads in the sand and mourn the gloom. We can't figure out what to say to ourselves, or tell our children, about a world in which so many terrible things happen. If we do not doubt, we choose to ignore. But pretending can't make it go away.

Maybe we ought to look more closely.

Consider the people in the Bible who came to Jesus to be healed. Most of them had stories that would make us want to hide in the closet. Their situations and problems were horrible. In some cases, their condition was disastrous because of the time and culture they lived in. Unclean people were completely ostracized by their culture, unable even to enter a place of worship. Other people had made life choices that were so despicable or frowned upon that the law required their death. Many were in torment—considered irretrievable wastes of time. Yet in all these horrible stories there appeared great good: Through God, death, disease, destruction, and evil became opportunities.

Why did it take forty-two generations to get from Abraham to Bethlehem? Why didn't the Father simply send his son to Eden to repair things right then and there? Perhaps it took that long for us to figure out what we were being rescued from. A friend of mine says the things that so often perplex us are simply designed to reveal our own futility. Jesus could not be a savior if there is nothing to save us from. Consider the great figures of the Bible. Most were abject disasters as human beings. Jacob, Moses, Rahab, David, Peter, Mary Magdalene, Paul—the list is endless. They weren't merely flawed. They were fatally flawed, but God turned their human catastrophes upside down for victory. And finally there was the cross, where the darkest hour of all creation became its brightest hope early one Sunday morning.

So when our faith is tested by what we see or read in the news, maybe tuning out is exactly the wrong thing to do.

I'm not suggesting that you watch or read the news more so those of us in the business can get more readers or better ratings. But I am encouraging you to look at the news differently. Maybe you'll hear a call to prayer. Maybe you'll find out about a problem that demands your attention. Maybe your disappointment will be replaced by divine anticipation. If you have children, maybe you'll be able to show them a single thread of promise in the fabric of fear. Hope might be hard to find, but it's never lost.

When the prophet Elijah was on the run, he took shelter in a cave. Alone, afraid, and distraught, the great prophet was suicidal. The whole world was closing in on him, and powerful people were out to kill him. It seemed as if everything Elijah had ever done was pointless and wasted. I imagine the mighty Elijah shivering in the darkness, cold and hungry, dirty and tired—his hair matted with filth and sweat, falling across his tortured face as streams of his tears fell into the dust. How his pitiful wails must have echoed through the caverns, and, as he sensed that there was no one near to even hear, how the gnawing emptiness in the pit of his stomach must have racked him with spasms of terror and abandonment.

Lightning ripped the sky and thunder crashed through the heavens—but God was not in the storm. Great tremors shook the earth, sending stones and dirt down onto Elijah's head—but God was not in the earthquake. Without warning, all of creation seemed to erupt with searing flame, as smoke and sulphur choked Elijah's hiding place—but God was not in the fire.

And then, God showed up. Then, says the Bible, there was "a still small voice" (1 Kings 19:12).

God speaks in many ways. He is not always noisy.

Let's listen closely, look past the headlines, and see.

1

One Little Line

Looking Past the Headlines

—⟨ɷɷ⟩—

Look, there on the mountains, the feet of one who brings good news, who proclaims peace!

Nahum 1:15 NIV

Nahum is not a happy book.

Written by Nahum the Elkoshite around 620 BC, the Old Testament book predicts the fall of the ancient city of Nineveh, the capital of Assyria. The Assyrian Empire had survived for more than 300 years, but its fall was imminent—and Nahum's prophecy would prove amazingly accurate in its detail. The book of Genesis says Nimrod founded the city on the banks of the Tigris River in northeastern Mesopotamia. The Bible calls Nimrod "a mighty man" on earth (Gen. 10:8), but that's not entirely a compliment. His name itself translates as "rebellion." Nimrod the Hunter, as we've come to know him, was more likely Nimrod the Obstinate.

A renowned warrior, Nimrod founded Babel and other ancient cities, crowned himself king, and likely created the first dictatorship. Jewish legend has it that Nimrod ordered the murder of more than seventy thousand children in order to kill the child chosen to return the people to God. Abraham survived, but Nimrod's own heirs continued the king's tyrannical ways with enormous success. God eventually sent Jonah to Nineveh in order to get the people there to repent, but Jonah himself so disliked the Assyrians because of their treatment of Israel that he initially ran away from the assignment. Even after Nineveh repented, Jonah hoped God would destroy the city anyway (Jonah 4:1–5). By the time Nahum arrived on the scene, Nineveh was at it again, and the final opportunity to change had passed.

Nahum's prophecies are brutal. Almost every sentence foretells the terrible darkness and destruction just around the corner. Divine wrath and judgment are in almost every line, and it all came to pass in the year 612 BC. When Nineveh fell, she fell very hard. The Babylonians and their allies cut up the Assyrian Empire for themselves, and today nothing is left of Nineveh but ruins.

And yet, right in the middle of all the bad news, Nahum quotes the prophet Isaiah. "How beautiful upon the mountains are the feet of him who brings good tidings, who publishes peace, who brings good tidings of good, who publishes salvation, who says to Zion, 'Your God reigns'" (Isa. 52:7). Smack in the middle of a horrible story of death and disaster stands one little line of hope, beaming from the hill.

Maybe Nahum was looking past the bad news. Perhaps he was looking beyond the headlines. Maybe he knew that the real story was the feet on the mountain—feet that would one day be nailed to a cross.

I am a television news anchor.

I can identify with Nahum. I'm one of those people who often seems to deliver nothing but bad news. I've been in broadcasting now for thirty-plus years. Some things you never get used to. I can't tell you how many times I've been on the set watching an especially nasty story unfold, and either heard my partner or myself say out loud, "That's the most disgusting thing I've ever heard!" And it is, until the next most-disgusting thing pops up.

Many people I talk to these days tell me they don't even crack open a newspaper, let alone watch the news on television. Who can blame them? It's vital for people to be informed if they wish to remain free, but most of what makes the airwaves these days is more often than not dismal or scandalous. In a curious way, that's the good news. Since news is by definition the exception to the rule, what we report and what you see is usually not the norm.

WBAP's Mark Davis is one of the most successful regional talk show hosts in the United States, and his theory is that the things that make something newsworthy are familiarity, oddity, or impact. People who do the right thing aren't usually newsworthy. No one slows down to watch a good driver, but let one person foul up on the freeway and every station in town will launch their news helicopters to get an overhead view of the accident scene. Of course, there are more than enough foul-ups on a daily basis to fill up hundreds of newscasts. Seeing the steady stream of foul-ups leaves the viewer to wrestle with a world that seems completely out of whack. The vile or heartbreaking seems commonplace, and the good appears completely forgotten.

Meanwhile, scattered among the downers is the occasional story of the sick child who has a happy ending or the neighborhood that bands together to help someone in need. Those things happen every hour and every day. People who love each other and are kind to each other and treat each other with respect don't make headlines because, thankfully, that behavior is still considered normal. Honesty, decency, sacrifice, duty, and honor still largely rank among preferred qualities in just about any culture. Most of these virtues still hold value.

Astrophysicists tell us that far off in space there are things known as neutron stars. At one time, they were regular stars, much like our own sun. As they consumed more of their own fuel, they expanded many times their own size. When that fuel was spent, these stars collapsed upon themselves. Their extreme mass pulls their atoms closer and closer together until they become fantastically dense. A piece the size of a matchbox might weigh millions of tons. Eventually, scientists theorize that they collapse to the point where they become practically invisible. Not even light can escape their gravity. The only way to know they exist is by the effect they have on everything around them. Their "weight" might be enormous, but their influence is completely out of proportion to their size.

It's the same with the news. We're used to looking for the huge. We often miss the things that are small. They might not seem important at the time, but tiny things can have more weight than we can imagine. I think a lot of the stories we cover are like that. The devil isn't in the details. God is. We miss the "still small voice" when we focus on the thunderstorm.

It's the good news that brings things back into balance. The fact is, good news threads its way through every story. Sometimes it's not immediately obvious. The word *gospel* means "good news," but I doubt there was anything "good" particularly obvious to the disciples as they ran for their lives at Gethsemane, or while Jesus's bloodied and broken body hung on the cross.

When I was a child, we played a game called "Hide in Sight." Whatever it was that we were supposed to be looking for was left right out in the open, but because our minds prefer the obvious, we looked right past the object of our search. It's the same way with good news. It's always there, right there in front of us. Pointing out the good news isn't always possible in a thirty-minute newscast. Time usually limits us to the train wrecks. Plus, the news cycle demands new information. We can't dwell on any one detail of a story for very long—even if that facet is invigorating and empowering. Plus, for reasons we'll talk about later, it's not always the reporter's job to point out the ultimate author of this good news. But if we watch the news with a different mind-set, the reporter doesn't have to.

A mysterious series of sniper attacks occurs near Washington DC. Buried under the speculation of who might be responsible and what kind of gun was used we hear about the Guardian Angels who volunteer to pump gas for people afraid to stand outside their cars.

The Mississippi River floods out thousands of our neighbors and millions of square miles, reminding us once again that she will never be tamed—but America responds with a generous heart that seems to be inexhaustible.

The driver or motorcycle rider who is tragically killed by a drunk driver on a lonely stretch of road thought of others even in death, and his or her transplanted organs provide life and hope for their recipients.

So with God's help and inspiration, this book is one small attempt to report a few stories and events I've covered personally in a different way. These conclusions are my own, so I encourage you to engage your own experience, study, and understanding. The world might not seem so hopeless the next time there's not much worth celebrating in the paper or on the newscast.

Anne Murray sings a song called "Sure Could Use a Little Good News Today." A little is all that's needed—maybe just one line in a story that we might miss entirely if we aren't watching closely. It's up to us to look for it. It might not be any bigger than a matchbox. But good news balances things out and tips the scales in its own favor.

Yes, Nahum wrote a book filled with terrible judgment and justice. But it's not that strange that this obscure Judean would include that one little bit of good news in verse 15. The name *Nahum* means "comfort."

2

In the Moment for God

A Church-Bus Crash outside of Dallas

—◦∿◦—

Through him we have obtained access to this grace in
which we stand, and we rejoice in our hope of sharing
the glory of God.

Romans 5:2

June 24, 2002, was a weekday morning. A convoy of
church buses was on its way from Metro Church of
Garland, Texas, to a youth retreat in Louisiana. The bus
leading the caravan was packed with youngsters. The
main highway from Garland to Louisiana is Interstate
20, where more accidents have happened over the last
few years than on any other stretch of pavement in the
state of Texas. On this beautiful summer morning, there

would be one more. I got to the station early. Almost from the second I walked in, the inter-office email was buzzing about a bus accident a few dozen miles east of Dallas, near the town of Terrell. There were reportedly several injuries and perhaps several fatalities. It quickly became clear that we were going to have to go live on the air with the story.

It only takes a few minutes to put on the on-camera makeup we have to use. Television reveals every little flaw, so wrinkles and dark eye circles all have to be covered. I put the powder on as quickly as I could and headed to the small set in the newsroom called the "flash-cam." There's a stool, a lectern, a camera—and not much else. The other stations in town already had helicopters taking live video from the scene, although ours was delayed in getting there. But no one needed another camera angle to see that it looked like the bus had exploded.

The bus had somehow swerved off the road onto the right shoulder and hit a concrete bridge support pillar. The driver's side of the bus had been pushed back at least a third of the length of the vehicle, with debris and wreckage scattered all over the highway and shoulder. At any accident scene, emergency crews place plastic tarps over the deceased to preserve dignity, and the coverings are easily visible at a distance. Even without those markers, it was painfully obvious that the driver must have been killed, along with anyone sitting on that side for at least half a dozen rows. News journalists are obliged not to speculate on such things as casualties until the information is actually confirmed, but when you've seen something like that enough times, you know. Perhaps you don't know the exact numbers, but you know someone isn't going home again. Worst of all is the thought that somewhere, someone who had a loved one on that bus is tuning in right then, and they're learning the terrible news from you.

My oldest son was on a church bus that morning. For a moment, I thought it might have been his bus. The likelihood was small, but the coldness of the thought gripped me. We simply didn't know whose bus it was. And yet there I was, sitting in my makeup with my microphone, expected to deliver this news dispassionately and professionally. We did our job, but with each second into our newsbreak, my voice became weaker. There were several of these newsbreaks through the morning, leading up to our noon newscast. I think I closed the last one by acknowledging a prayer vigil that was already beginning back at Metro Church.

The gathering at Metro Church was a prelude to a news conference church leaders were hastily assembling. The injured were still arriving at area hospitals, and already there were remote trucks and live crews setting up to get reaction at the church itself. I'm sure no one with a camera or a notepad expected the reaction they got.

As I watched one of the television monitors in the newsroom, a group of several church members emerged from a side door of the church building and walked to the bundle of microphones already set up for the statement, which would be followed by the usual questions and answers. Even newspeople make fun of some of the questions that get asked in situations like that. We don't mean to, but someone always seems to ask something inane, such as "How do you feel?"

One of the men in the group stepped to the microphone to address the reporters. He welcomed them and asked for a moment of prayer. And then something happened that I've never seen in nearly thirty years of broadcasting. The man opened his prayer with thanks to God for being merciful, expressing a deep concern for the injured and lost. He thanked God for all those who had come to pray, and for the emergency crews who were still on the scene extricating bodies from the twisted steel. And then he said, "Father, we thank you for the many members of the media here today, and that they may have their questions answered. And Lord, if your grace and power is revealed to even one person here because of what's happened today, then we give thanks."

I was speechless.

Many times and in many situations I have seen the grieved turn to God in prayer. I've seen them do so in private and before cameras and microphones. But I had never seen anyone acknowledge the hope that those of us in the media might benefit spiritually. Yet here was a church that was just barely beginning to deal with an overwhelming loss, refusing to lose sight of God's ultimate will. They didn't say, "God, we're glad this happened," or "Lord, we're happy to have this chance." These people were stricken, totally devastated by their loss—and yet so connected to God that they were able to say, "We don't understand, but we give thanks."

That afternoon, I sat down and wrote the people of Metro Church a letter. Reporters and news anchors aren't supposed to get involved with the subjects of their stories, and we're surely not to take sides. But I was sure at the time, and I'm sure right now, that God used them to touch more than just one person that day.

Several weeks later one of the pastors called to thank me for the letter and invited me to speak to their Saturday morning men's group. Whatever I said that morning is not nearly as important as what they showed me—the same faith in God that Metro Church had shown to the media. These people were that way all the time. I met a man who was about to leave on a dangerous mission trip to North Korea and China. Another man had reclaimed his life from lost nights spent in bars and nightclubs. I'd known him from those days and saw a sort of redemption I was only beginning to experience. One of the men there looked at me with sad eyes and a quiet confidence in his face. His attitude never betrayed his intense pain—he was the father of one of the victims.

These people were devoted to following God in their everyday living, so they were equally ready to do the same when the storm clouds of tragedy came.

In the days after the accident, the demands of time and newsworthiness quickly edged out the prayer of Metro Church. Live comments can't be edited, but as the story unfolded, new information eventually relegated the church's prayer for others to the margins, and soon it disappeared altogether. It isn't really a conscious decision to edit out things that are religious in nature. It's just that our job is to gather the new developments and breaking news. Replaying the church's prayer over and over would not have served that purpose. But of everything that happened that day that truly mattered, perhaps there was no bigger story than a group of people who looked past their own pain and followed the will of God.

Where did their prayer come from? Why was it so effective? Jesus talks about that in the book of Matthew. Jesus warned his disciples that the job he gave them would leave them as vulnerable as sheep among wolves. They would be dragged before kings and courtrooms, where they would be hurt and humiliated. He tells them to be as wise as serpents and as innocent as doves. But he also tells his chosen not to worry: God is in control, and when disaster strikes "what you are to say will be given to you in that hour; for it is not you who speak, but the Spirit of your Father speaking through you" (Matt. 10:19–20).

On one hot summer morning, a small group in Texas looked past their own pain and toward others. The weeks and months ahead would be difficult, to be sure. The cost to this small church family was great, but in no way could it dim the reflection of Christ they managed to convey in those first trying days. Heartache and loss are an inseparable part of life—but they could not defeat humble faith. For at least a few moments, while struggling through an ocean of grief, the people of Metro Church saw the world through the cross and showed us Jesus.

Lives were touched by their example—and if for no other reason than that one day, I believe God will remember them for their faithfulness.

✳

On February 14, 2003—almost eight months to the day from the accident that had claimed the four young lives from Metro Church of Garland—a chartered church bus traveling north from Temple, Texas, went out of control in heavy rain just south of Waco. Thirty people, mostly senior citizens, were on that bus, headed for a Bill Gaither Family concert in Dallas. Five people aboard the bus were killed in the crash, plus another two in a second vehicle.

Later that afternoon, Bill Gaither spoke with more reporters outside the concert arena. Gaither quoted an old gospel song written in 1834 by Edward Mote, the son of a London pub owner. Mote would later say, "My Sundays were spent in the streets, filled with such ignorance that I did not even know there was a God." A cabinetmaker to whom Mote was apprenticed took him to church, and many years later, Mote gave the world these words:

> My hope is built on nothing less
> Than Jesus' blood and righteousness.
> I dare not trust the sweetest frame,
> But wholly lean on Jesus' name.

Eight months earlier, God apprenticed me to the people of Metro Church through a simple, humble prayer. Like Mote, I am quite sure that before that moment I had scarcely known there is a God. I had learned a system of belief, but to believe is not the same thing as to *know*. My small difficulties paled before people going through unspeakable grief—people who thought first of God's blessings and of blessing others. These people *knew*, and they passed it on. Many things have changed in my life since that day because of one simple prayer.

I was the member of the media they had touched.

3

When the Words Won't Come

Amber Hagerman and the Amber Alert

—⟨⟨⟩⟩—

Where were you when I laid the foundation of the earth?
Tell me, if you have understanding.

Job 38:4

For what seemed like the eighth time in just two weeks, the Amber Alert had saved another child.

The Amber Alert System is a very simple idea. When the authorities suspect a child has been abducted, local radio and television stations immediately interrupt regular programming to broadcast details of the abduction, along with a description of the victim, the suspect, and the vehicle involved. The broadcasters get their information by fax from the local police or law enforcement agency. Some states now use computerized highway signs that usually warn of construction or detours to relay the information right to drivers on the road. It's been remarkably effective, possibly saving the lives of children in every state where it is used. Today, another child was found thanks to the Amber Alert.

I was there for the event that launched it, a cold and snowy morning in January 1999 when they found the body of Amber Hagerman.

She'd been riding her bicycle when she was taken. Some witnesses said they saw a black pickup truck in the area of Amber's disappearance, and police searched for that truck for days. Possible suspects were taken in for questioning, and criminal profilers were brought in to try to decipher the psychology of the kidnapper. Local radio talk shows buzzed with horror and speculation. Investigators searched everywhere they could think of, while the experts surmised that Amber's kidnapper must have taken her to a familiar place. The thought that Amber was already dead wasn't spoken in public or on the air. But we knew it was likely, in spite of the hope Amber's mother bravely showed each day in front of a phalanx of cameras and microphones. The sad fact is that most kidnap victims are killed within seven hours of their abduction. Some suspicion fell upon family members, since statistics also show that family members are overwhelmingly behind child abductions—the non-custodial parent, or the jealous aunt, to name a few.

The area was paralyzed for days, while people hoped and prayed. Members of the media became fixtures in front of Amber's home. And then they found her body.

The details of what had happened to her were largely kept out of the headlines and news stories. In Texas, we stick to the discrete when reporting on the death of a child. The graphic details aren't necessary, and the families certainly don't want to hear them—even though many media outlets have now relaxed that unspoken prohibition.

Amber's body was taken to a modest funeral home in Arlington, not too far from where she'd been kidnapped. For days, the site of her abduction had become a growing shrine of stuffed animals and flowers. In the days before her funeral, many of those mementos were moved a few blocks away to the chapel where the final good-byes would be said.

The night before Amber's funeral, I decided to go to the funeral home. The chapel was filled to overflowing with teddy bears, stuffed animals, toys, and flowers. In the center, near the front, was Amber's blue casket. The lid was open, and the line to pass by stretched to the back of the room. Soft music played in the background. I took my place in line and gradually worked my way to the front of the room. The closer I got, the more emotional I became. As a father, I can scarcely imagine the pain and terror of losing a child. I doubt anyone really knows what that's like unless they've been through it.

Amber's face was peaceful, and the pale blue satin surrounding her looked comfortable. Being a little girl, she would have noticed that, along with the vast sprays of flowers that embraced her resting place on all sides. Maybe journalists aren't supposed to do this sort of thing, but at the time I was only a talk show host, so it seemed forgivable, if not permissible. I took a moment to reflect, gathered myself, and turned to leave. Amber's mother, Donna Whitson, sat in the front row. I leaned down to take her hand, and although I can't recall the exact words, it was something to the effect of "we will not give up." To this day, I wish I could have come up with something a little more comforting. Thinking back, it seemed an arrogant statement, as if somehow I spoke for the offended masses everywhere and the parents themselves. Amber's mother offered a muffled thank-you, and with tears gently welling from her eyes, extended her hand to the next mourner.

Thoroughly drained, I walked outside to catch my breath. A local reporter named Sean Rabb was standing on the sidewalk. For years, Sean has been one of the most dogged and productive reporters in our market. He's scored countless exclusives for his television station; even when he's covering a school board meeting, he always seems to command attention. He has a deep voice and a signature sign-off—a melodramatic pause between his station's call letters, with an elongated pronunciation of the word *news* at the end. I don't know if he was waiting for his camera crew or just taking a minute to escape the weight of it all. Not even funerals are sacred or private if it's a story everyone is talking about.

We greeted each other, and then neither of us said a word. It seemed like several minutes passed before one of us could muster enough strength to mutter a single word. I think I simply said, "Sad."

Sean inhaled deeply and exhaled his response. "Yes," he replied, drawing out the "s" out of exhaustion. I knew he'd been covering Amber's story from nearly the beginning. There was no guessing how many times his pager had gone off in the previous days, or how many times he'd been called to his station in the middle of the night to chase a new lead or a potential hope. To see it all end this way had to be crushing for a man like Sean, who sees the humanity in the stories he covers. The seesaw effect of a story like this one is an unspoken source of great stress to reporters. The closer they get to the subject of their reports the more they are drawn into the crests and troughs of an emotional tide. When a story ends tragically, often they literally feel like they've washed up on the beach, completely spent.

We stood there looking helplessly at each other, at the ground, and at the sky. I remember Sean was wearing his usual topcoat against the cold night air, but the stylish fedora he often sported was missing. It was not an occasion for keeping one's head covered. After several more minutes of silence, a question came to my mind. It was an honest question, born of sheer confusion.

"What do we say?"

I wasn't really expecting an answer, but I got one.

"We've just got to give this one to God, brother," said Sean.

I knew it was true of course, but over time, my sense of the statement's impact has grown. Here we all were—family, friends, observers, reporters, ordinary folk who had merely watched the story unfold—standing in the very dark shadow of just how cruel and evil the world could be.

A child lay dead mere feet from where we were standing, and yet, from hope, conviction, or both, Sean acknowledged the fact that no matter how hard any of us might have tried to fathom it all, there was simply no sense to any of it absent God. He didn't mean that Amber's death was preordained, and he didn't mean that God wanted it to happen. He didn't mean there was any deep, hidden meaning to it all, or that good things would come of it. All Sean meant is that we are simply unequipped to understand on our own—and that we shouldn't even try. This one was beyond understanding, beyond our control, and the only option left was to hand it over to God. Trying to figure it all out or trying to answer the question of "why" was only going to lead to total frustration. It happened because there is evil in the world, and there is no figuring that out. Sexual predators and their psychology aside, the only answer to darkness is light, and even the best of us can't offer enough illumination.

It's been years since Amber Hagerman was buried. The Amber Alert System is going nationwide. The little girl will never be forgotten, and her name is now associated with people who will do everything they can to make sure other children are found, safe and whole. Not too many miles from where she was kidnapped and later found, a local landowner set aside a small patch of earth, now known as the "Garden of Angels." It was informal at its beginning—a mere series of crosses, each bearing the name of another lost loved one, mostly children. Teddy bears and flowers piled up over time, until the memorial eventually outgrew the original site. Now, the Garden is landscaped and tended with loving care. As of this writing, fifty-five crosses stand in that garden, and the families of the dead come to remember, reflect, and ask their own questions.

Amber Hagerman's killer has never been found. I suppose we in the media more or less kept the promise I offhandedly made to Donna Whitson that night. Maybe through support of the Amber Alert, we haven't given up. But whenever our newscast or the headlines are filled with another inexplicable death of a child, I recall the words of a very tired reporter, spoken in both sadness and hope. The nature of our business prevents us from offering Sean's advice as we tag our stories, but for me, these words have echoed in my mind over the years. There've been times when I've wanted to say it on the air, and many more times when I've struggled to actually believe it.

Our inability to understand doesn't mean we're not intelligent. It's amazing just what we do know these days. The things we take for granted today were only the imaginings of Jules Verne, H. G. Wells, and Isaac Asimov. George Lucas and Stanley Kubrick took those daydreams to the movie screen, but they were still mostly just popcorn fantasies. When I think of Captain Kirk's little communicator, I look at my cell phone. It wasn't long ago such things seemed completely far out. The paralyzed actor Christopher Reeve may walk again soon. He's always insisted he would, but most of us probably winced the first time we heard Reeve say that around his breathing tube. It no longer seems impossible. God knows what tomorrow will bring.

But knowledge is not the same thing as understanding. What we cannot or will not understand, we question. If the answers don't satisfy us, we demand. When the reasons still don't appease, we often become cynical and condemn. C. S. Lewis wrote about that very subject in *God in the Dock*. Injustice and unfairness offend us, anger and enrage us, so we indignantly storm the gates of heaven, make our arrest, press charges, indict, and hand God over for trial. We make ourselves the judge and put the Creator on the witness stand. We cross-examine the Almighty and treat him as a hostile witness. We are absolutely certain that we are entitled to an explanation. We've all asked the questions. "How could God do this?" or, "What kind of God could allow this?" One can almost hear the old serpent himself, saying "Just do what I tell you, and you'll have your answers! You *deserve* them!"

But "How unsearchable are his judgments and how inscrutable his ways! 'For who has known the mind of the Lord, or who has been his counselor?' 'Or who has given a gift to him that he might be repaid?'" (Rom. 11:33–36). God can take our questions, but he expects our trust. He says, "Be still, and know that I am God" (Ps. 46:10).

Our place is not the judiciary. We have no business on the bench. We're just not qualified. God is the judge, not us. He wrote the law books. It's his court. There was no justice in what happened to Amber Hagerman, and her killer is still out there. But out of something unspeakably evil, great good came. Is that what it took? I don't know. I hope not. I'd like to think not. But I think Sean Rabb is right.

Sometimes, all we can do is give it to God.

4

I Don't Even Know How

The Wedgewood Baptist Church Shootings

——◦◦◦——

When my soul fainted within me, I remembered the LORD;
and my prayer came to thee, into thy holy temple.

Jonah 2:7

"I don't even know how to begin telling this story." The
reporter who said this was sitting on the concrete steps
outside the Wedgewood Baptist Church in Fort Worth,
Texas. The words were meant for no one in particular,
although everyone in the media there could appreciate
the sentiment to one extent or another. Just hours before, a man named Larry Gene Ashbrook had invaded a
Wednesday night prayer service carrying guns and pipe

bombs. Of the 140 or so people inside, 7 were wounded, and 7 more were dead.

Shootings like this seemed somewhat commonplace in 1999. For a while, it seemed like the papers and newscasts were filled with similar reports on a daily basis. They always involved a loner or a small group of outcasts taking their frustrations out on the innocent and unsuspecting. Larry Gene Ashbrook fit the profile perfectly. Almost a recluse since the death of his father, investigators later found Ashbrook had papered the walls of his room with strange writings, scraps of paper torn from Bibles, and disturbing drawings. He'd even sealed his toilet by pouring cement into the bowl. He was on prescribed medication, although he seemed to have stopped taking it for some time. At the time of the shooting, witnesses told reporters that Ashbrook had entered Wedgewood's main auditorium on September 15, 1999, shouting a flurry of obscenities and insults directed both at Christianity and the people praying in front of him. Ashbrook had been raised in a conservative Christian church; later, some people tried to ascribe his rage to that upbringing. All stories need bad guys, and some people tried to make Ashbrook's youthful church life the villain. Thankfully, it didn't catch on. Ashbrook was a very sick man who did a very evil thing.

There were miracles that night. Witnesses told how both of Ashbrook's pipe bombs failed to detonate, saving many lives. Most of his gunshots missed their targets. One girl with scoliosis is said to have survived because the curvature of her spine displaced her vital organs, putting them out of one bullet's destructive path. One story had it that as Ashbrook moved back toward the rear of the sanctuary, he spotted a young girl praying between the pews. Witnesses say Ashbrook raised his gun to fire, but at the last moment, turned and walked a few feet away, where he fired a final round into his own tortured brain.

Nothing like this had ever happened in Fort Worth before, and the local media pounced. Live trucks and helicopters were dispatched immediately, and before long, the networks and satellite trucks had arrived to carry the story to the world. Almost immediately, high-ranking police, fire, and government officials were on the scene to address reporters. The wounded were barely on the gurneys before the questions started to come. The first news conference was held that night, with the police and fire chiefs, the city spokesman, and a representative from the mayor's office. Both the relevant and the perfunctory questions were asked. They all must be, since our job is to ask the questions the public would but can't. How many people were dead? How many were wounded? Was there only one shooter? The harder questions about what actually happened inside and who the shooter was would come later. The question of "why" might forever remain unanswered, and the reporter sitting on the front steps would have to come up with his own words. That was his job.

In the days that followed, there would be public memorials and private prayer. Governor George W. Bush and Fort Worth's mayor, Kenneth Barr, made a private trip to pray with members of the church. The official memorial was held in a local football stadium and was attended by tens of thousands. It was broadcast on local television and rebroadcast both on television and on the Internet. Most of the seven victims had been young people, and thousands of youth groups across the country sent condolences to Wedgewood.

The church's ministers and pastors appeared on an amazing variety of network television shows, and their testimony was beamed to millions around the world. Many say that the way the Wedgewood church handled the situation, their witness of Christ in a time of unbearable pain, led unknown numbers of people to the cross. One caller to a local Christian radio station reportedly said, "I don't know what those people at Wedgewood have, but I want it." The deejay led the caller to Christ right then and there, live on the air. Many of the stories were undoubtedly anecdotal. Many more were authentic and life changing.

I don't know if the reporter on the steps ever figured out how to begin to tell this story. Sometimes sterling prose or dramatics actually work against us and all we can do is go with the facts: "A gunman opened fire at a Fort Worth church tonight, killing seven people and wounding seven more."

A few days after the shooting, I had the privilege of interviewing Dr. Al Meredith, the senior minister at Wedgewood Baptist Church. The floor of his sanctuary was still stained with blood, but Meredith projected a serene quality—evidence of what the Bible calls the peace that surpasses all understanding. It was clear he was stricken with grief, but possessed of an inner strength born of faith. We were live on the air. It was early on in what's called the "development" of the story. It's always good to get a live interview with a principal player in any story, but it's even better when you get them at the start. Journalists know that it's at such unguarded moments that the answers will be the most compelling and poignant.

During the conversation, I said something to the effect of, "Pastor, about the seven who died . . . " I never finished the question. Dr. Meredith interrupted me almost immediately.

"There were eight who died."

It took a second for me to register the statement.

Pastor Al Meredith was including Larry Gene Ashbrook.

In spite of the terrible evil that had been visited on his congregation, Al Meredith saw the carnage through the forgiving, loving eyes of Christ: There *were* eight who died. That humble Baptist minister put it more eloquently than I ever could. In the eyes of God, the Larry Gene Ashbrooks of the world are no less loved than the world's most pious saints—and none of us is really worthy of that love.

I think that kind of attitude was the reason Wedgewood Baptist Church received tens of thousands of supportive emails, letters, and cards in the days and weeks after the shootings. People saw that this ordinary suburban church had the courage and faith to glorify an extraordinary God, and they were drawn to it. Maybe that was how that reporter and all the rest of us should have begun to tell the story. Meredith's inclusion of Ashbrook was unsettling, but it was the truth.

Eight people died. Their names were Cassie Griffin, Kim Jones, Kristi Beckel, Justin Ray, Shawn Brown, Joseph Ennis, Sydney Browning—and Larry Ashbrook.

The first thing many of us want to do is assign blame to someone or something. It's easy when someone does something horrible: We thank God we are not poor sinners like they are (Luke 18:11) and feel better about ourselves. But God tells us repeatedly in his Word that we are not the final arbitrator—he is. That's his job, not ours. My youngest son once asked me who was going to heaven. I thought about the question for a while. All the different theologies on the subject raced through my mind, and I thought about how to answer the question in a way that a small boy might understand. All I could come up with is, "I don't know, but God does, and whatever he decides is alright with me." Frankly, most of us are probably glad we don't have to make that decision—but that doesn't mean we don't try.

In news, we confront the unfairness of life every day. Poor families lose everything they have in a fire. Corporate executives cheat stockholders and still keep their million-dollar mansions. Highly paid athletes abuse drugs or girlfriends yet are still worshiped by millions because they can carry a football or sink a three-pointer. Sick children suffer and die before they've ever had a chance to even live. Each day, the media parades evidence that life is not fair. But salvation isn't fair, either. Thank God it's not. If salvation were fair, none of us—not one—would receive it. We talk about injustice and fairness, but it's not justice we're after. We want *mercy*.

Thankfully, God's in the mercy business.

It's tough to do what Pastor Meredith did. It's hard to look at the despicable acts of a Larry Ashbrook and think for a minute that God felt about him just the way he does about me. But if God offers us mercy, how can we do anything but offer mercy to others? That's not easy to swallow. There are a lot of people out there whom we have a hard time loving. But that's what God does. We ask for mercy, and he allows people to come into our lives who shoot up churches, kidnap children, fly airplanes into skyscrapers.

Forgive them? See them the way God does?

Are you kidding?

They simply don't deserve it.

But then, neither do we. Two thousand years ago, God offered mercy and people spat in the battered face of the Lord of the Universe. But his offer still stands.

There were eight who died.

Is it easy? No. But it is Jesus.

"Who is a God like thee, pardoning iniquity and passing over transgression for the remnant of his inheritance? He does not retain his anger for ever because he delights in steadfast love. He will again have compassion upon us, he will tread our iniquities under foot. Thou wilt cast all our sins into the depths of the sea" (Mic. 7:18–19).

After all, the first two spoken words recorded from the cross were "Father, forgive."

It's risky business to follow that example. It's tough to show mercy to those who do things we hate. It's hard to forgive those who hurt and mortally wound us. The world doesn't think like that, but Jesus did.

5

The Unspoken Call

Delta Airlines Flight 191

—∾∾∾—

I was thirsty and you gave me drink, I was a stranger and you welcomed me, I was naked and you clothed me, I was sick and you visited me, I was in prison and you came to me.

Matthew 25:35–36

August 2, 1985, was a typically hot and humid summer day in Texas. The so-called "Metroplex" of Dallas-Fort Worth and all the attending suburbs bustled with activity. The afternoon rush hour was starting to peak, with tens of thousands of people hitting the freeways at about the same time. Overhead, a few late summer cumulonimbus clouds gathered, teasing us with the promise of a late summer shower. Dallas-Fort Worth is always a busy place—a fact best reflected in the giant airport nestled between the two cities. There are always dozens of planes in the sky over Dallas-Fort Worth, and that day, they seemed to play hide-and-seek with the increasing clouds.

Several hundred miles to the east, Delta Airlines flight 191 was over Louisiana, headed from Fort Lauderdale to Los Angeles, with a stop in between at DFW Airport. The plane had departed Florida just after four o'clock eastern time, carrying 167 passengers and crew. It had been an uneventful flight, but as the giant L-1011 crossed into Texas airspace, a growing monster lay in waiting.

An August rain in Texas is a rare and appreciated thing. Often, the land goes from late June all the way to autumn without much rain. Sometimes the rain comes as a gentle summer shower. Other times the sky explodes with sudden fury as towering thunderheads quickly reach forty and fifty thousand feet. A small cloud on the horizon can become a supercell thunderstorm with blinding speed, producing torrential rain and incredible wind within an extremely small area. Winds on the ground can gust up to seventy miles per hour, producing extraordinary downdrafts within the shaft of the thunderstorm itself. One such downdraft produced winds over eighty miles an hour in the 1990s, canceling a Texas Rangers baseball game when officials feared light standards over the stadium might fall. A dying thunderstorm in the 1950s produced an outflow of wind, which compressed and superheated as it rushed from the northwest toward the town of Meridian, where longtimers there say temperatures near Lake Whitney climbed above 120 degrees within a few minutes, withering cotton in the fields and causing car radiators to overheat and boil. But the extremes on the ground are nothing compared to the unimaginable fury within the clouds. Although springtime is considered severe weather season in Texas, even a small thunderstorm in summer can be capricious and deadly.

As Delta 191 approached the normal flight path into DFW, air traffic controllers alerted the cockpit crew to a thunderstorm forming off the north end of Runway 17L. The prevailing winds in Texas are from the south, and 191 would land into the wind. Radar returns in the tower confirmed the developing weather situation, but the picture was deceptively incomplete. White puffy clouds concealed an incredible updraft in a relatively small thunderstorm near the north end of the airport: Inside the darkening clouds was a storm capable of expending more total power than 100 nuclear reactors. Planes inbound for DFW would have to fly dangerously close to the jaws of a beast.

All was relatively normal as 191 approached the airport. The crew had been warned about the storm, and a Lear jet just four miles ahead of the big airliner reported no unusual problems. Within minutes, the picture changed dramatically. Passing through 800 feet, the huge L-1011 began to pick up speed, although no one was pushing the throttle. A tailwind enveloped the aircraft, dropping 191's relative air speed. Just as a boat must travel faster than the water around it to maintain control, an airplane must fly faster than the air around it to keep from losing lift and altitude. The tailwind was a clear indication of potentially catastrophic wind shear—a whipsawing condition no pilot wants to face and few planes can handle. A strong tailwind can instantly reverse into a mighty headwind, making stable flight impossible. As 191's airspeed dropped even further, the crew slammed the throttle up as far as it would go. Somewhere around 119 knots—just above a stall—the crew pushed the nose over in a frantic attempt for more speed and control, but an indescribable downdraft hammered the plane like a giant fist, driving her straight into the ground.

Delta 191 bounced down in a small field just north of the airport and then came down on a small car traveling down Highway 114. The tiny car was totally crushed by the number one engine, and the driver was decapitated. With one engine now disabled, the plane's power was out of balance, and it careened at more than 220 knots toward two giant water tanks just across the highway.

No plane of this size had ever crashed in Dallas-Fort Worth. In fact, no plane of any kind had ever crashed at DFW Airport. Within seconds, emergency and rescue crews swarmed over the crash site. It was close to the highway, which made getting there easier, but a tremendous downpour from the storm had turned the field where the plane finally came to rest into a quagmire. The gigantic water tanks had ruptured, mixing more water with the jet fuel and blood. Getting to the crash site through all that was nearly impossible—both physically and emotionally.

Radio had the news first, but television crews arrived with unbelievable speed. Reporters assigned to the story stood knee-deep in mud as emergency crews worked feverishly behind them. The gargantuan tail section of the L-1011 appeared in every live shot, a dramatic suggestion of the utter devastation present at the scene. The tail section of an L-1011 is several stories tall. The problem with television is that no matter how big something is, it never looks as big on your set as it is in real life.

Six o'clock newscasts expanded from their normal thirty minutes to an hour, and just kept on going from there. Hospitals were filling up, although there were far fewer survivors than there was space to receive them. Still, the emergency response and whether it was adequate was also part of the story. Friends and loved ones waiting inside the terminal had to be told. Airport officials hustled them to a secure, private area—out of the range of the prying media. It was all part of the story. Of the 167 people on board Delta 191, more than 130 were dead. Families elsewhere had to be contacted and their stories reported. There was much to be done.

I don't remember anyone on radio or television making any special requests of the public. There was so much to cover and so many angles of the story to pursue that I honestly don't think anyone thought of it. It's not that it wasn't important or wasn't needed—it's just that there was never a concerted call for a public response. But the response came. Within hours, thousands of people lined up at the area's major blood banks. All the media did was report what had happened. Folks just showed up. Regular people knew what they needed to do, and they did it.

In the years since the crash of Delta flight 191, safety measures have been put in place to prevent other jetliners from becoming ensnared by wind shear. New technology has made it possible for air traffic controllers and meteorologists to spot trouble well before a plane is in too deep. Even cockpits are now equipped with their own version of Doppler radar. Flight crews drill over and over in state-of-the-art simulators about how to handle microbursts and dangerous winds.

I drive past the crash site several times a week. Every time I do, I think of the people who showed up at the blood banks. I don't know what they were doing that afternoon when they first saw or heard the news, but I know they must have been busy. They must have been leaving work, or preparing dinner, or just spending a few minutes with each other—when they were moved. They saw the story on television or heard it on the radio, and many didn't need to be told what to do. They responded.

I am a big Bruce Springsteen fan. Springsteen and his legendary E Street Band released "The Rising" in 2002, written in response to September 11th. You can relate the subject matter of "The Rising" to things well beyond 9/11; the themes of loss, sacrifice, and longing are eternal. In spite of the hurt Springsteen manages to capture in songs like "You're Missing," "Empty Sky," and "My City of Ruins," the listener is left with a tremendous feeling of hope and encouragement.

Not too long after "The Rising" came out, I saw a fascinating interview with Springsteen in which he talked about his inspiration for the album, and all of his music.

48

People, says Springsteen, are incredibly brave. They're brave at work, at home, in their families, and with their co-workers. They often do things they don't know they're capable of doing, performing great good for no recognition or gain. Many times, they don't even give it a second thought. According to the singer, it's simply the best part of what we really are, showing through. Lincoln spoke of that as he prepared to heal the nation after the Civil War, appealing to "the better angels of our nature." It's the kind of thing that doesn't make a lot of newscasts, but it does make the world a much better place. But where do these angels come from?

God made us in his own image (Gen. 1:26). All the emotions we have come from him. He feels joy, sadness, tenderness, disappointment, anger, jealousy, love—and compassion. Hence, there is something in each of us that reflects our Creator, often in spite of ourselves. It wants to go home, back to the place where it came from. We may not even be aware of our imitation of him. We may attribute that spirit to something else. His seed is deep within us, and his fruit demands to appear. Like God, that fruit shows up where it's needed most.

Did all of those people who donated blood on that hot August day know that they were answering the better angels of their nature? I think not. They just did what they did and didn't stop to ask why or think about it. Are we always aware that all good things are directly from God (James 1:17)? No more than the Samaritan on the road from Jerusalem to Jericho.

The Jews of Jesus's day hated the Samaritans, who came from an area near what is now the town of Nablus on the west bank of the Jordan River. The Jews considered Samaria both godless and lawless, and its people weren't even considered neighbors. In fact, Samaritans were so despised that the young lawyer who asked Jesus about receiving eternal life could not even bring himself to *say* "Samaritan" (Luke 10:37). Jesus chose the central character of his story for a purpose. In the parable, a traveler is beaten, robbed, and left for dead by the side of the road. A priest walks on the other side of the road to avoid him. A Levite does the same thing. Then a Samaritan comes by, bandages the victim's wounds, takes him to an inn, cares for him, and pays for his further care. Jesus asks the young lawyer and everyone else there which of the three passersby was a neighbor to the victim. The story doesn't suggest that the Samaritan ever asked himself that question.

God placed part of himself inside us. It's the good within us. It is there regardless of our station in life or our relationship with him. That seed is there, no matter how hard we deny it or try to bury it beneath our own pride, guilt, or fear. He calls to it and for it, delights in it, wants it to grow, longs to see it reveal its flower, and desires to see its fruit. He wants us to be all that he made us to be, full-time. He wants us to lay down ourselves, to lay down our lives for others. Through that surrender, he knows only then can we find genuine joy. It's what we were made to be. He wants us to stop hiding in the garden and be reconciled to him. He wants his children to share in his glory.

He's looking for us even now.

He is, after all—a *father*.

Fathers don't hesitate. Neither do neighbors.

6

Blessed Are the Meek

An Afternoon with Ernie Banks, Buck O'Neill, and Jimmy Carter

—◦◦◦—

> The meek shall obtain fresh joy in the LORD.
>
> Isaiah 29:19

It was going to be a very big day.

It was springtime, and baseball season was in full flower. The station I worked for at the time not only was the flagship station of the Texas Rangers Radio Network, but our studios were located in the Rangers' home stadium. Designed to recapture the classic designs of the good old days, it sits squarely between Dallas and Fort Worth in Arlington, Texas. The structure rises like a giant granite temple from what was once Texas prairie.

Few buildings nearby rival it in size or presence. Step inside, and you are transported to a time when baseball was the poetry of a nation. A mixture of old Tigers Stadium in Detroit, Ebbets Field in Brooklyn, and Fenway Park in Boston, the atmosphere is both modern and antique. You know you're in the twenty-first century, but you swear you see Gehrig, Robinson, and Williams warming up on the sideline.

The radio station's main broadcast studio sits at street level, with huge windows allowing a great view of either the sunrise or a growing crowd bustling along the sidewalk before game time. The conference room sits immediately above the visitor's bullpen, and the back door of the station opens directly into the bleachers in left-center field. On many days, I would arrive at work early to sit in those bleachers to enjoy a cup of coffee. I could hear the echoes of history as I visualized great games of the past as the morning sun began to stream through the portals of the upper deck.

It is impossible to go to work in a bad mood when you work in a ballpark.

We were to have three interviews that day. The first was with the great Ernie Banks. Banks grew up on the sandlots and playgrounds of Dallas before joining the Chicago Cubs. A terrific second baseman, he was also a tremendous slugger and ambassador for the game. His Hall of Fame career is exceeded only by his hall of fame personality. Banks's magnetism and enthusiasm are infectious, and his trademark phrase of "let's play two!" is a great motto for anyone who loves what they do and doesn't ever want to stop. I grew up while Ernie

Banks was still playing, and the thought of meeting him caused my heart to race.

Our second interview was tied to Banks. Buck O'Neill may be one of the finest human beings I've ever met. Buck is in his nineties now, but you'd never know it, either by talking to him or looking at him. The only give-away is an incredible wisdom gained from a lifetime of experience. O'Neill spent most of his baseball career in the Negro Leagues. Although he played with and knew legends such as Satchel Paige and Josh Gibson, the major league color line was still intact, and some of the finest athletes of any age were forced to play in a separate league, sleep in different hotels, and dine in different restaurants. Despite their greatness, they were subject to insults and degradation. Yet when Buck O'Neill speaks of America and her national pastime, there is a twinkle in his eye and a smile in his voice. O'Neill remembers the hard times, and while he acknowledges the truth, there is not one iota of bitterness in him—only joy. Most Americans became familiar with O'Neill after filmmaker Ken Burns produced a documentary on the game of baseball, using Buck to tell a great portion of the game's story. On television, O'Neill comes across as the grandfather we all wish we'd had. He'd managed and scouted both life and baseball with incredible success, and I was going to get to sit at his feet and listen.

The third interview was perhaps the most exciting of all to me. Former president Jimmy Carter had just written a new book and was on a promotional tour. Since leaving office, Carter has been involved in many causes, but far more frequently, he's to be found hammering nails and building homes for the homeless or teaching Sunday school in Plains, Georgia. Carter's book was comprised of reflections on his faith, and I was excited at the chance of talking to someone who clearly views his relationship with God as far more important than the most powerful office in the world. It would have been exciting for me to interview any former president. There's something about the office that transcends the man who holds it, and I've felt my insides do flips when watching a presidential motorcade pass—no matter who was in the backseat of the limo. It's as if all that we are as Americans is condensed into one individual, for better or worse. Here was a man who had labored under that heavy yoke.

The Secret Service had been in a few days before to inspect our studios and make sure of our building's security. Former presidents have lifetime Secret Service protection, although most have a much smaller detail after they leave office. The agents were very thorough. Large windows and easy street access were concerns, even though President Carter had been out of office for several years.

The day of the interview arrived, and local police closed an area of the street immediately outside our offices. Bright orange cones blocked off a stretch where the president's entourage would arrive, so that Mr. Carter could quickly jump from his car and sprint directly into our studio. He was scheduled to arrive just before eleven, which gave me two hours to spend with Ernie Banks and Buck O'Neill, but Mr. Carter had also been known to arrive early.

The first part of the show was the stuff memories are made of. Talking baseball with the likes of Ernie Banks and Buck O'Neill is like talking religion with Billy Graham and the Pope. When there are so many stories to hear, the smart interviewer doesn't interrupt. We took dozens of calls from listeners, and almost as many of the staff came in just to sit and listen. Both men were visiting the ballpark that day to attend the regular noon luncheon sponsored each month for fans by the Rangers organization, so they had to leave about eleven. Neither Banks nor O'Neill knew that a former president of the United States was coming, and when the time came, Ernie darted upstairs after signing several dozen autographs. Buck O'Neill stayed behind for a minute or two to say hello to a few more fans in the newsroom.

On cue, President Carter's mini-motorcade slid deftly into the reserved area on the street. It had been pre-arranged with the chief of Mr. Carter's security detail that he would spend a few minutes greeting the management of the station and then would come inside the studio for our interview. There would be a chance to take pictures, since just about everyone wanted a picture with an ex-president. The baseball greats were to head out one door while the president came in another. If our guests even saw each other, they would pass only briefly in the hall.

At the top of each hour, the station carried network news. That ended at five minutes past the hour. Ordinarily, guests come into the studio a few minutes before the end of an hour to exchange hellos with the host. But by the end of the network newscast, there was no sign of

Carter. After three minutes of local news, still no sign. Radio talk show hosts are largely a neurotic bunch, and when there's no guest in sight as the newscast gets to the local weather forecast, we start to fall apart. I decided to go outside and see why the president was keeping me waiting.

There was the former president of the United States, glowing like a schoolboy, listening to Buck O'Neill spin his magic in the newsroom.

Most people might think it would be the ballplayer paying rapt attention to the former commander in chief. I can't even begin to imagine the stories a president might tell—if he could. I'm all but convinced that the day a president is sworn into office, someone—maybe the head of the CIA or the outgoing president himself—walks into the Oval Office with two stacks of files. The first is very thick, and the second is very narrow. Maybe even a single folder. The bearer of the files sets the first down on that big oak desk and says, "Mr. President, this is how people think things are." Then he sets down the single folder and says, "Mr. President, this is how things *really* are." I'm convinced the contents of that smaller file are why almost all presidents go into office with a head full of dark hair and leave with a mane that's gone completely white. Having the reins of liberty and national security largely entrusted to one's own hands is heady stuff. Once out of office, there surely must be at least a few things that would make for great water-cooler conversation starters.

But not that day. The former chief executive was all ears.

56

Jimmy Carter was the fan, and Buck O'Neill was the object of his admiration. It was like watching a five-year-old in front of Santa Claus.

Baseball does that to a lot of people. It carries us back to days of innocence and joy. It reminds us of endless summer days with locusts chirping in the trees and lawn sprinklers chattering next door. It reminds us of faraway places we only heard about on the radio, and playing catch. What we saw that day wasn't a former president talking to a former ballplayer. What we saw was a fan—a genuine admirer—talking to his hero. We saw a man who once held the most powerful office in the world unconsciously and instinctively humbling himself before a fellow human being who had his own stories to tell. What we saw was the biblical definition of humble—empty of self.

A well-told story illustrates President Carter's inner fiber. When former Vice-President Hubert Humphrey passed away in 1978, Richard Nixon returned to the White House. It was his first visit since leaving the Oval Office in resignation and disgrace. Much of the country still regarded Nixon as an embarrassment, if not a crook. Few people knew how to react to his presence, and the ex-president stood alone off to one side. After a few minutes, President Carter entered the room and began greeting the assembled dignitaries. Then he saw Nixon. Without hesitation, the sitting commander in chief strode across the room and extended his hand to his predecessor. The two embraced, and for all to hear Carter said, "Welcome home, Mr. President. Welcome home." As a writer for *Newsweek* later observed, "If there was a turning point in Nixon's long ordeal in the wilderness, it was that moment and that gesture of love and compassion."

I'm not entirely sure what it takes to make a great president. Courage, conviction, creativity, and an abundance of confidence don't hurt. Humility isn't one characteristic that gets mentioned very often. But one day in an office hallway, deep beneath the bleachers of a ballpark, we saw what it takes to make a good man.

7

Real People

Troy Aikman and John Elway

———

Do nothing from selfishness or conceit, but in humility
count others better than yourselves. Let each of you look
not only to his own interests, but also to the interests of
others. Have this mind among yourselves, which is yours
in Christ Jesus, who, though he was in the form of God,
did not count equality with God a thing to be grasped,
but emptied himself, taking the form of a servant.

Philippians 2:3–7

One of the most enjoyable experiences in my business
is getting to meet people who turn out to be just as nice
in private as they seem to be in public.

Many people who achieve even the smallest bit of fame or notoriety quickly let it go to their heads. Some people retreat behind handlers and go so far as to hire people to say "no" for them. Other people become downright mean, ordering subordinates around as a master might command his slaves. Anyone who has been in radio, television, motion pictures, the recording industry, or print for very long has seen all kinds. In fact, many people who are in the media can easily be placed in one of the aforementioned categories themselves.

Some of us have alternated back and forth.

One of the most embarrassing snapshots of my career was taken a very long time ago. North Texas is home to the largest community of military retirees in the United States, and at the time, it was also home to Carswell Air Force Base and a Naval Air Station. The owners of Billy Bob's Texas, which bills itself as the largest honky-tonk in the world, decided to hold a huge party to celebrate members of the military. I was the house deejay/rodeo announcer/master of ceremonies. For entertainment that evening, they hired no less a luminary than the great Bob Hope. Prior to the show, special guests and staff could meet Mr. Hope and have their pictures taken with him. When my picture was finally developed, it was painfully obvious that this was not a moment I would wish to remember. There I was, standing with one of the greatest entertainers of our time, talking his ear off. Instead of listening to a man who could impart wisdom gained from countless years onstage and in the public eye, I was doing all the talking. The precise look on Hope's face can best be described as, "Who is this guy?" I never gave Hope the chance to let me know whether he was the real deal or not, and I'm not sure I even thought to ask him any advice. I've never chosen to hang that picture in public.

It might be possible to blame that episode on the fact that I was young and stupid at the time, but there've been many such episodes since, and that excuse gets old after a while. On the other hand, I've seen extremely famous people at a similar age behave with unbelievable humility and kindness. One of my favorite stories involves former NFL quarterback and future Hall of Famer Troy Aikman. Thanks to the fact that I worked for the Cowboys flagship radio station at the time, I've had the pleasure of knowing him since he arrived in the league from UCLA. In the mid-1990s, Aikman owned Dallas: Three Super Bowl championship rings, charisma, boyish charm, a ton of money, and an almost magnetic appeal for women might have corrupted anyone else his age. But Aikman has always known who he is and has never let his fame come between himself and reality.

Once, a man I knew was going through a terrible divorce. He knew his two children were suffering and decided they might need some inspiration. Knowing that Aikman had gone through a similar heartache, the man wrote the famous quarterback to see if he might drop a card to his boys. Instead of a card, the boys got a heartfelt, genuine, and moving letter in which Aikman revealed how he identified with the boys' fears and emotional needs. With the exception of those whom the man eventually told, no one ever knew what Troy had taken the time to do. Despite Troy's relentless and untiring support for good causes, the vast majority of his generosities remain unpublicized. He is a far better person in private than he is in the spotlight.

Another great illustration involves another famous NFL quarterback. The Denver Broncos were in town for an exhibition game. It was a steaming hot summer night at Texas Stadium, and again, my job permitted me to be on the field. By the fourth quarter, most of the people who'd come to see the game had made haste for the relief of any place offering air conditioning. The players couldn't wait to shed their bulky equipment, hit the showers, and head out; under such conditions, players often don't wait for the final gun to begin their exit. Broncos quarterback John Elway was already a legend, although his Super Bowl success wouldn't come for another few years. He was already considered one of the greatest quarterbacks to ever play football, and he certainly didn't need an exhibition game to tune up for the regular season. Elway started the game but spent the entire second half on the sideline. With about two minutes to go, there was no doubt he was looking for the exit like everyone else.

As the game wound down, I was walking near the end zone, where seating is provided for those with disabilities. The view isn't bad, but what's even better is that it brings fans up close to their heroes. For many fans with special needs, that opportunity often means more than words can express.

As I passed the special seating area, a woman motioned me over. Next to her were three small children of about the same age who were not only in wheelchairs, but custom-made wheelchairs meant to accommodate profound disabilities. I recognized the family from a story I'd done a few years earlier. The three children all suffered from a form of dramatic muscular degeneration—a usually fatal condition. All three children were smiling broadly, and their mother was waving a piece of paper in my direction. Her question was simple and direct.

"Would you take this to John Elway? He and my son Tommy are pen pals."

I muttered something to the effect that I would try, smiled, and headed toward the Broncos bench. I wasn't sure that I could do what this mom wanted since there would be a crush of people around Elway, and I didn't have the right security pass to get that close. There's a very clear boundary around the players' area because the NFL doesn't want reporters or microphones in there until the game is over. I thought I'd give it a shot, because it seemed so important to the mother, and I had given my word.

There was less than a minute to play by the time I got to the Broncos bench. Unbelievably, Elway was sitting alone and unguarded. High-profile athletes can be a little jumpy when anyone approaches them from behind and taps them on the shoulder, but Elway calmly turned and looked. I handed him the note and said, "John, there's a woman down there in the end zone with three kids who wanted me to give you this."

Elway took the piece of paper, gave one quick look, and immediately jumped to his feet. Without hesitation, he started off in the direction of the end zone as the game came to an end. As the gun sounded, Elway broke into a full trot.

It was an amazing scene. Every other orange jersey in the place was headed for the tunnel at the opposite end of the field. The showers and cold air were waiting, followed by the trip back to their luxury hotel. The buses couldn't leave until everyone was on them, and they sure weren't going anywhere without the star player, but the star player was going to make them late. He had three children in wheelchairs to visit.

I didn't follow him or try to get a story out of it. I just watched. Elway's jog slowed, and even from fifty yards away, you could see the smiles of the mother and her children. I'm not sure how long Elway stood there, but I do know everyone else had left the field by the time he turned toward the players' tunnel. It might have been ten minutes; perhaps it was longer. But how long he stayed there chatting with his pen pal and the little boy's two siblings really wasn't the point. The most captivating moment was the instant when he stood, looked, and knew where he had to go.

One day, at a house in the town of Capernaum, Jesus decided to have a little heart-to-heart with his disciples. On the road through Galilee, Jesus had overheard the twelve discussing which among them was the most important. All were earnest, sincere, and dedicated—but there seemed to be a small question of who ranked where. Jesus began by asking them what they'd been talking about. When no one had the fortitude to answer, Jesus took a seat in the home as a child played nearby, and he taught an unforgettable lesson.

"'If any one would be first, he must be last of all and servant of all.' And he took a child, and put him in the midst of them; and taking him in his arms, he said to them, 'Whoever receives one such child *in my name* receives me'" (Mark 9:35–37, emphasis mine).

Great football players watch game films for days, draw up a game plan, work on it endlessly in practice, and have all the faith in the world that it'll work on Sunday. But then comes the kickoff. It's no longer theoretical at that point. You have to buckle on your helmet and strap on the pads. You have to take what you know and what you've practiced and put it into action.

You have to stand, look, and make the play.

8

Both Sides of the Coin

Oklahoma City Bombing

———

For the waves of death encompassed me, the torrents of perdition assailed me; the cords of Sheol entangled me, the snares of death confronted me. In my distress I called upon the LORD; to my God I called. From his temple he heard my voice, and my cry came to his ears.

2 Samuel 22:5–7

The reporter and I stood there speechless.

It was April 20, 1995. The Alfred P. Murrah Federal Building was gone.

It had happened on the morning of the previous day just after nine. I was just beginning my daily talk show when wire service alarms began to go off all over the newsroom. Something terrible and huge had just happened in Oklahoma City. No one was sure what it was. At first, there were thoughts of a giant natural gas explosion or perhaps a nearby oil tanker. It quickly became obvious that it was something far more sinister.

By the time I got off the air at noon, station management had decided that the next day's show would be broadcast live from Oklahoma City. An engineer, one of the station's reporters, and I would go. By eight o'clock that evening, we were waiting for our plane at the airport.

I'll never forget that night. Our plane took off during raging severe Texas weather. Tornado and storm warnings were up all across the area. It seemed fitting.

The plane landed at Will Rogers Airport in Oklahoma City. A car from an affiliate radio station was there to pick us up, and we began the ride into downtown. The area around the bombing site itself was closed for blocks, so we had to park at least a half-mile away from the scene. Power had been disrupted by the blast, and nearly all the lights of downtown were off. The night air was crisp and surprisingly cold. As we parked behind a darkened building, we could see our exhaled breath illuminated faintly by a distant glow in the sky.

Within a quarter mile of the Murrah Building, glass and broken plaster began to crunch under our feet. Before us, a pale light coming from over the tops of the buildings began to intensify. The crunch of our footsteps through the debris was the only sound. No one spoke.

Suddenly, we rounded one last building, and there it was: The glow we'd seen was coming from racks of emergency flood lamps that surrounded the site. The lighting rendered the scene simultaneously colorless and vivid. The Murrah Building was more of a skeleton than a structure, an effect that was further impressed on the mind by the bathing light. There were emergency and law enforcement vehicles everywhere, and many news units and satellite trucks. Cameras and faces were all pointed toward the steel and concrete cadaver where so many had gone to work that day. At its base was a giant pile of collapsed floors, disintegrated walls, and destroyed lives.

From where we were standing, creatures that seemed to be ants swarmed over the pile. As we drew closer, the ants could be seen on their hands and knees, carrying plastic buckets. Even closer, the ants became rescue workers and searchers, painstakingly looking for survivors and victims. Not only were they digging, they were also listening. All activity would stop at the slightest hint of faint breathing or scratching sounds, or at the groan of weakened girders and concrete floors that constantly threatened to give way. If the disaster seemed large on your television set, it was forty times larger in person. It was so huge in its impact that the heart could not absorb it. There was no scale by which the thing could be measured—at least not then.

By the time night turned into day, even more people had gathered. Governor Frank Keating was granting interviews, as was Senator Don Nickles. The swell of news units and live trucks hadn't even begun to crest, and the network morning shows were all present to take the images and emotions to all corners of the world. Broadcast outlets sent their best.

The vast majority of journalists in this country are every bit as affected by the stories they cover as is their audience. In spite of what many people think or how reporters are often portrayed in the movies, journalists are not bloodthirsty sharks constantly on the prowl for ratings or a scoop. The competition is intense, and like every other job, we usually advance based on our ability to deliver the goods. But journalists and reporters also take their stories home with them, and often, they have to deal with their own emotions alone. There is no chaplain for these troops, and yet on the air or in their writing, they are obliged to be as emotionless and impervious to pain as possible. Not everyone can adhere to that standard all the time. Sometimes we can handle it, and the next time we can't, particularly when it comes to stories the size of Oklahoma City.

Thankfully, there were images of heroism and sacrifice to draw from. There was the doctor who had helped extricate a woman from the rubble by amputating her leg. He performed the operation while resting on his belly and elbows, in a crawl space no bigger than a very small steamer trunk. There was no anesthesia, and the surgery was done with a knife. The entire time, the mass of rubble above him threatened to fall and seal both doctor and patient in death. The story was widely reported and became famous, as did many other stories in the days after.

Many of those stories received extensive coverage, but some did not. Some went unnoticed or couldn't be given their due because there were simply so many stories to tell. The Navajo firefighters who came when no one asked and spent countless hours in the broken building. The people of Oklahoma City, who poured out their hearts with coffee, food, and care for the searchers and the media. The volunteers from all over the United States who came and did whatever they could, etching forever the image of the bloodied and torn hands of the rescuers and searchers who had literally clawed their way through the leather fingers of their heavy gloves.

Many things have been said and written about the bombing in Oklahoma City. How we remember that day and its aftermath is mostly a matter of choice. But selfishness and hate did not win on that day or in the days after, nor have they ever won.

When I think of Oklahoma City, I don't think of the building, the bomb, or even Timothy McVeigh. I recall the bloody hands of those who came, those who searched, and those who saved.

9

Serving Two Masters?

The Relationship between Faith and Media

—⁓⁓—

No one can serve two masters; for either he will hate the one and love the other, or he will be devoted to the one and despise the other.

Matthew 6:24

A lot of people are convinced that the news business is totally godless, if not altogether anti-Christian. I've been around the broadcasting and news business for more than thirty years—and nothing could be further from the truth.

There are many people in journalism who have no active spiritual life, either by choice or through attrition. Reporters are naturally skeptical, and that's a good thing, but the job can make some more cynical. Others have reasoned it out to their intellectual satisfaction that there either is no Creator or, if there is, he is not in active control.

But the fact is, many (if not most) of the people working in the news media today profess at least some kind of faith. The role of a free press is by definition somewhat adversarial, so none of us can afford to take much at face value—but that doesn't mean an absence of values.

Despite what many of my colleagues prefer to believe, there is institutional bias. That's how it has always been. Newspapers and networks, like any other human enterprise, operate according to certain philosophies. In areas of the country where intellectualism and inquiry are valued above all else, suspicion, especially toward anything based on faith, is rewarded at least to a degree. And people of faith, being human, often give their critics plenty of ammunition. Indeed, our country was founded partly on deep reservations regarding "established" religion. Any journalist—whether he or she possesses a professed belief or not—faces quite a spiritual wrestling match. We all do.

Ideally, the journalist or reporter has but one job—to report. It's up to the audience to decide what the news means. Editorial writers, columnists, commentators, and art critics offer their own take because that is their expressed purpose. But in straight news, it's not our job even to *accidentally* "promote" one viewpoint over another, whether Republican versus Democrat, or believer versus nonbeliever. Professionally speaking, whom you vote for or what god you worship is your business, not mine, and stays that way unless your vote or religion is an integral part of the story. But even when it is integral—even when the story involves a priest accused of misconduct, or an imam accused of inciting his followers—it is not up to me to color the information you get with my own opinion or faith. At least, that's the way it's supposed to work.

Listeners often add their own spin and make assumptions about what we're saying. Many times people who consider themselves "conservative" will detect something in a news story that to their mind is "liberal,"—and therefore inherently bad. And vice versa. In the human sense, perception is reality—even when it is entirely incorrect. The choice of a word or the arch of an eyebrow must mean something, but it can easily mean different things to different people. Back when I hosted a talk show, I once received two voice mails. Both calls related to the same subject I'd been discussing that day, and they were back-to-back on the recording. The first caller accused me of being a screaming liberal, while the second anointed me a redneck conservative. Two people had heard the same thing, and their reactions had been polar opposites. I saved those two calls for years.

But the viewer or reader's perception is far from being exclusively at fault. Some media bias is unintentional. A lot of it is the result of outright laziness. Just the other day, I received a phone message from a viewer who was upset that I chose to call the president "Mister." What she did not know was that the president's name is often written without any title at all—and that I was the person who had inserted the words *president* and *mister* into the copy in the first place. Otherwise, I would have simply called him by his last name. Most newsrooms have a policy of giving appropriate title when it comes to the commander in chief—no matter who happens to occupy the White House, or whether we like that person or not. But in the second reference, only the last name is generally used. As far as this viewer was concerned, I was being entirely biased and disrespectful to the president. As far as I was concerned, I'd slipped it in because I didn't want to refer to him by last name only.

The most common evidence of bias cited is what many people call "tagging." How many times have you seen a story in which certain believers were referred to as "fundamentalist Christians"? Perhaps they do believe in the fundamentals, and perhaps they don't. In fact, I can't quite tell you what the "fundamentals" are. Only the individual knows what he or she believes, and like any other group of people, get two of them in a room and they probably won't see eye-to-eye on everything. But it's handy to pile the whole bunch together under one label. We do it constantly, and often, unconsciously. It saves a lot of time, and it effectively conveys an image to the mind of the viewer or reader. Unfortunately, one of the best ways to take away anyone's identity is to stick him or her with a label. It's hard to avoid when you have only thirty seconds to tell the story, so good writers keep an eye out for generalizing or labeling. Tagging reduces people into categories. It's unfair. But it still slips by.

Another trap is called "re-tracking." A reporter in a faraway city puts together a package on a certain story. That story is put on the daily satellite feed, available to every subscribing station. Subscribers get the video and the script in a nice, tidy package—ready to go. All a local station has to do to localize that story is have one of its own reporters or anchors simply re-track it by re-recording the audio using his or her own voice and the original script. Unless the viewer is very astute, it appears that the local reporter has done the story. It's an accepted practice in an era of smaller newsrooms, limited resources, and budget considerations, but big stations do it too. Many local reporters will double and triple check their scripts before they read anything, but some don't. And when they don't have time or inclination to check the copy for accuracy or slant, an error or bias may be repeated. It's a dangerous dilemma. On the one hand, newscasts and newspapers need to be filled with credible "fed" material or wire service copy. News consumers demand and expect the news. But the trade-off is that errors, inaccuracies, incorrect perceptions, or bias may be repeated over and over. Frankly, I can't stand re-tracks. In the first place, someone else did the work. In the second, I'm essentially being asked to be a parrot. Thankfully, many news directors feel the same way and resist using re-tracks.

Another pitfall—especially in medium and smaller markets—is the overburdened, underexperienced producer. The individual putting together the late news may be an award winner, but chances are good that the person producing the noon newscasts or morning shows is fairly new to the business. He or she simply might not have either the time or the background to know everything that can slip by. So that individual writes a story about Navy fighter pilots—not knowing that the Navy refers to its fighter pilots as *aviators*. Maybe he or she inserts a banner at the bottom of the screen reading *United States marines*—not knowing that the word *Marines* is always capitalized. Maybe the reporter has video of an Air Force F-16 Falcon, or an Army M1-A2 Abrams main battle tank—but refers in his script to an F-15 Strike Eagle or a Bradley Fighting Vehicle. You can see the problem: In the space of a few sentences, that producer would have convinced any viewer with knowledge of these four of America's five service branches that he or she was a complete idiot, or worse—that the station had contempt for the military.

One common pitfall involves the young writer facing a story about property taxes—I've faced this one with a few people. Younger people usually lease instead of own, so their property tax is buried in their rent. They never see it and never have to write the check themselves. It wasn't too long ago that they lived at home and their parents were paying property taxes, so when they hear there'll be a cut in the tax *rate*, they translate that into a tax *cut* and write as if homeowners are about to save some real money. Of course if you've ever owned a house, you know its value can climb enough to offset a cut in the tax rate. You may wind up paying even more. When that happens, you'll remember the bozo on television who told you that your taxes were going to go down. Chances are you won't watch that bozo anymore.

If I'm not very careful with the words other people put in my mouth, that bozo will be me.

When it comes to intense matters of personal belief and faith, the risks are even more combustible. Newsrooms and journalists have to be *very* good and *very* conscientious. For example, you and I might both attend the same congregation or denomination, but that does not mean we share all the same beliefs, and it's inaccurate for anyone to suggest that we do. I'm a member of the Church of Christ. Like Episcopalians, Lutherans, Catholics, Methodists, or anyone else, not all of my beliefs are identical to those of my brothers and sisters. But it takes too long in the average news story to sort out all the differences. It's more convenient for journalists to just lump everyone together. That's not only inherently inaccurate, it also tends to irritate those who are being lumped. It's not difficult to imagine that eventually that entire group of people feels that the media is not only against them, but also *after* them.

Let's look at the media mess over the Southern Baptist Convention's decision to emphasize the Bible's admonishment for wives to "submit" to their husbands. Although Southern Baptists are one of several different brands of "Baptists," it wasn't long before the words "Southern Baptists" disappeared from a lot of scripts, to be replaced by "Baptists." Not all Baptist branches were party to the decision, but some news stories made it sound that way. Moreover, most journalists weren't Bible majors, so we didn't pay much attention to what Paul actually meant by the word "submit," and our stories didn't do much explaining. But "submit" is a word that tends to create a lot of stir, so we used the controversy to attract viewers without getting very far into what the rest of the Bible says about how husbands ought to treat their wives—that would have taken a lot more effort, and it would have diffused a lot of contention. So the whole thing was painted in primary colors. It wasn't malicious, it made great headlines, and it got a lot of people talking—but it wasn't necessarily balanced. It also wasn't a product of anti-Christian bias. The furor was more a product of convenience than conspiracy, although that didn't make it any less destructive.

How many times have you heard a reporter or talk show host refer to the Supreme Court's decision "banning prayer in public schools"? The phrase is short, compelling, and punchy—and it causes a strong emotional response. It's also factually wrong. The Supreme Court of the United States banned organized, sponsored prayer in public schools, meaning those schools subsidized by taxation. Since we are compelled to pay taxes, we must be careful that taxpaying individuals of different minds should not be compelled to support prayers with which they may not agree.

To recall Thomas Jefferson, compelling a man to worship at an altar in which he does not believe is tyranny. I don't want the money I'm obliged to give the government supporting an atheist group, any more than my friend the atheist wants his money paying for the public address system over which my prayer is prayed. Plus, the justices never said people can't pray in public schools. Like the old quip, I have two sons, and they take tests—so I know they pray. Maybe even with their friends around the flagpole, or in the hall. But those prayers are not sponsored, endorsed, or led by people on the public payroll. Nevertheless, you'll hear the media consistently and lazily refer to "banning prayer" in school all the time. That mischaracterization is now accepted as fact and has caused great division and anger among millions of Americans.

Another example is the Ninth U.S. Circuit Court of Appeals decision that the Pledge of Allegiance is unconstitutional. Of course, the justices never said any such thing. So far, the Pledge is perfectly constitutional. You can recite it however you choose. But in a public venue supported by public money, the Ninth Circuit Court ruled the phrase "under God" unconstitutional. The basis: the founders' insistence that there must not be even the slightest chance of an official government endorsement of one religion over another. Europe's history of combining state and religion is the very reason the founders chose to separate church and state. Even so, where that line should be drawn can be argued between thinking and passionate people. But the ability to even have that debate is greatly lessened when people in my business fire off the phrases "since the Supreme Court ruled against prayer in school," or "the Ninth Circuit Court found the Pledge of Allegiance to be unconstitutional." In the rush to fit in all our words and pictures, facts can get lost. Unfortunately, it makes it easy for the casual observer to think there is a cultivated denial of God in government, or at least a purposeful effort to report only those things that suited the reporter's own beliefs.

But there's another dilemma for journalists who do profess faith. If the newscaster or reporter is a Christian, that discipleship is supposed to color everything he or she says and does. Most of the stories that make the news aren't pleasant ones. Those of us who look at the world through the cross would like to find the good in even the worst cases, and we'd like to tell you about it. Very few journalists, no matter what they believe, enjoy telling a story that leaves little or no hope. Editorial decisions about how to approach a story usually come from a consensus reached around a conference table surrounded by reporters, producers, editors, and news directors. But when we get back to our keyboards, the choices are not just professional—they are, by definition, personal. Which words do I choose? Where do I draw the line? What's the message? In theory, the story itself dictates how it will be told. Good training says just give the facts and let the audience decide. It's all but impossible to remove human feelings and emotions from most stories, especially when the story is gut-wrenching—but that's often precisely when it is absolutely imperative for your words to be devoid of any personal feelings at all. Yet in those private moments when the real editorial decision is made in an individual's heart, we all must confront fact versus faith.

Does the believer try to find something uplifting in the middle of despair? If it's there and it's obvious, we'd all like to, whether we are believers or not. But something positive is often hard to come by. When a woman drowns her own children or an act of hate takes the lives of thousands, Jesus isn't always easy to see. It's not our job to introduce faith or hope into our scripts independent of the facts. It's not our job to steer you in any direction.

It's supposed to be our job to simply inform—nothing more. So how can any believing journalist serve both objectivity and God?

The Bible is pretty clear on the subject of submitting to authority, and workers honoring their masters. Considering there are many viewers in our audience who hold different beliefs, the Bible is also resolutely against putting stumbling blocks in the paths of others. My employer expects my work to be devoid of personal bias. Moreover, the audience has the right to *not* hear what I believe.

And most of all—thankfully—God doesn't depend on what I do to reveal himself.

Most every newsroom I know of has its own "style book" or relies on the style book provided by the Associated Press, detailing the accepted ways to refer to various public officials, titles that may apply to private individuals, proper grammatical usages, and so on. For believers, our style book is God's Word. But how do we reconcile being in the world but not of the world (2 Cor. 10:3)? More than likely, it's an issue for you where you work as well. Maybe you also have questions about when it's appropriate to render to Caesar or to God. Is it "Do not be conformed to this world but be transformed by the renewal of your mind" (Rom. 12:2), or "The faith that you have, keep between yourself and God; happy is he who has no reason to judge himself for what he approves" (Rom. 14:22)? If there is a blanket solution—a magic bullet that I could whip out to solve the issue of when to speak up and when to sit down—it is this:

"Do not be anxious how or what you are to answer or what you are to say; for the Holy Spirit will teach you in that very hour what you ought to say" (Luke 12:11–12).

God. He's the ultimate managing editor.

And the cross always reveals itself—no matter what.

10

Courage under Fire

The Assassination Attempt on President Ronald Reagan

———ᦖᦘᦗ———

A cheerful heart is a good medicine.

Proverbs 17:22

In the early 1980s I was working as a disc jockey at a dying country and western radio station. The place had once been a mighty force in the market, but time and corporate neglect had whittled the legend down to a tax write-off in some obscure loss column. The on-air studio was always staffed by a disc jockey, but on the other side of the glass sat an abandoned newsroom. Perhaps twenty editing positions and typewriters sat idle, gathering dust where an entire staff had once worked to gather news.

The teletypes chattered nearby, producing wire copy the deejay occasionally checked for weather forecasts and news bulletins. We paid little attention to that room unless we had a long record on the turntable, and country records are notoriously brief. It doesn't take a lot of time to say "she left me and I'm going drinking," even with two or three choruses.

One day around lunchtime, the alarms on the teletypes went totally berserk. Two or three bells meant something like a severe thunderstorm watch. Five were more serious, such as a tornado warning or important breaking news. Ten bells meant somewhere, something life altering for everyone had happened.

Ten bells were repeatedly sounding, and wire copy was spilling furiously onto the floor. I put on the longest record I could find and scrambled into the newsroom.

"AP-Washington DC—President Ronald Reagan was shot today outside of a Washington DC hotel."

The words took a moment to sink in and then pounded me into the ground.

I'm old enough to remember the assassination of President Kennedy, but I was only a child when that happened. Now I was an adult, with twenty years of the American experience under my skin. My reaction to this news was swift and instinctive: Was the president badly wounded? Was he alive? What did this mean? The news was exploding across the wires, but the details were still sketchy. And before I would be able to get any of those answers, I'd have to go in the next room and deliver that news, alone, to an audience that would be just as shaken as I. It was my first job in a large market, and I had been hired to introduce songs by George Jones and Ferlin Husky. I was not prepared for this.

The words gathered in my throat as I opened the microphone but were choked off as I began to speak. Shock and disbelief overwhelmed me. It was completely surreal. The words forced their way out, with a promise to deliver any updates as they came in. Within minutes, country and western music was given the day off: Information and speculation flowed in nonstop from the nation's capitol.

Over the next few days it became clear that Reagan would survive. He had been wounded far more severely than we knew at the time, but timely medical attention—along with his physical strength and positive disposition—had saved him. Of all the things from that dark period, something Reagan reportedly said to his beloved Nancy in the halls of the hospital still resonates with me:

"Honey, I forgot to duck."

A lot of people have ascribed Reagan's statement to his actor's gift for good timing. But many more saw it, and still see it, as something deeper. There are people who have such a positive outlook that even when they are confronted with life-and-death situations, they still manage to keep their chin up—and in doing so, lift everyone around them. It's amazing how tears of horror can suddenly be turned into tears of laughter with just the right words. Reagan grasped that, intentionally and intuitively. I can't imagine anyone who has heard that quote who hasn't wished that they would have the same presence of mind in a similar situation. But I believe that presence of mind comes from the presence of peace within.

Ronald Reagan had his critics, and perhaps history will offer an even clearer picture of his overall impact than we have now. But the man knew who he was. That knowledge was reflected the day he was hit by Hinckley's bullet, it was reflected throughout his long career of public service, and it was certainly reflected in his loving letter to the American people announcing his long journey into the mists of Alzheimer's. Sometimes it was reflected with courage, sometimes with tenderness, and sometimes—perhaps at the most important times—with humor. If someone staring death right in the face can crack a smile and lift the spirits of those who are by the stretcher and not on it, then perhaps we don't need to be afraid either. We can look beyond our anxiousness and begin to trust.

I've reported a lot of life-altering stories since then. Every time one crosses the wires and I wonder how I'm going to choke out the details, I think back—and realize that as bad as things sometimes seem, they probably aren't as bad as I think they are.

D. Elton Trueblood certainly knew that. Without question, the great author, educator, philosopher, and theologian influenced the lives of millions of people, inside and outside of the church. Trueblood was born in 1900 and lived for 94 years. A lifelong member of the Society of Friends, or Quakers, Trueblood was a wonder. His sermons generally lasted only twenty minutes, and he could finish on time without a watch or clock. He spoke without notes and believed no book of significance needed to be longer than 130 pages. Trueblood cited Abraham Lincoln as one of the most influential people in his own life and wrote *Abraham Lincoln: Theologian of American Anguish*. The book has been read and quoted by many a subsequent president. Trueblood also authored some of the most colorful language in religious debate. Sobriquets such as "churchianity" and "religiosity" are Truebloodisms; sayings such as "the world is equally shocked at hearing Christianity criticized and seeing it practiced" carry as much weight now as when Trueblood first conceived them. In fact, Trueblood's definition of faith may be the finest ever offered: "Faith is not belief without proof, but trust without reservation."

One of Elton Trueblood's best books is entitled *The Humor of Christ*. If you have a copy, you're lucky, because the book is out of print now and hard to find. If you are able to get a copy, hang on to it. If you feel compelled to loan it to a friend, write your name inside and require collateral. Elton Trueblood understood that Jesus knew how to smile.

Ever squint at the speck of sawdust in someone else's eye while a two-by-four was sticking out of your own? Ever dipped your fingertip in your diet soda to remove a gnat while a Clydesdale horse floated elsewhere among the ice cubes? Ever take your Coleman lantern home and test it by firing it up and putting it under your bed? Visualize for a second trying to stuff Bill Gates through the eye of a sewing needle.

The prideful weren't the least bit amused by Jesus. In fact, the more Jesus revealed them for what they were, the angrier they became. The more they waved around the rules, the more Jesus lifted up the Ruler. But we become like them when we place our faith in our own understanding rather than God. In fact, God can't even use us until we reach the *end* of our own understanding. Job learned that lesson the hard way when God answered Job's whining with question after thundering question: "Where were you when I laid the foundation of the earth? . . . surely you know!" (Job 38:4–5). Some readers look at those words and come away with a sense of terror, but to me, they seem almost endearing. They sound exactly like the words of a frustrated parent quizzing an impetuous child about why he put the cat in the refrigerator or stayed out an hour past curfew. The truth is, our understanding is worthy only of ridicule—Jesus smiled in the face of their frustration and anger, and exposed them completely.

The world's great humorists know that laughter is one of the most effective weapons for deflating evil. Charlie Chaplin's *Great Dictator* and Mel Brooks's *The Producers* took on despotism and tyranny. Mark Twain and Will Rogers took the starch from many a stuffed shirt. Cartoonist Thomas Nast almost single-handedly destroyed the political gangsters of New York City's nineteenth-century "Tammany Hall" organization. But when evil is deflated, it isn't *devalued*. The sicker we are, the more cure we need.

President Reagan's words that day didn't just lift his own spirits. They lifted the spirits of a nation.

Not long ago, I covered a special graduation ceremony for a young woman named Emily Hunter. Emily was seventeen years old, and in her junior year at a local high school. Not only was she a star student, she was a star athlete—the first freshman ever to make her school's varsity soccer team. Everyone who knew Emily talked about her determination, dedication, and most of all her upbeat personality. She needed all those attributes.

Emily had a very rare form of cancer.

The young lady endured more than twenty surgeries, including six procedures on her lungs alone. In spite of radical chemotherapy to scald the disease from her system, Emily insisted on attending class as much as possible. When doctors were forced to amputate her right arm, shoulder, and collarbone, Emily tried out for the varsity soccer team again—and made it. She continued to work tirelessly in the community and at the hospital and clinic where she encouraged her fellow patients. As her body grew weaker, her resolve grew stronger. Everyone around her could see that she was losing physical strength fast, but even on her worst day she kept her sunny disposition. A freckled smile masked the terrible pain as she pressed on toward her dream. More than anything else, Emily wanted to graduate from high school.

And time was running out.

There was no way Emily could wait until spring. Through her horrific struggles Emily had managed to keep a near-perfect grade point average, so with help from her family, school administrators hastily prepared a special commencement. It would be held in the high school's main auditorium, complete with the school's entire orchestra and chorus. They would sing the alma mater and play "Pomp and Circumstance," just as if it were a routine graduation.

Emily Hunter died just a few days short of her graduation.

The night of her graduation, Emily's prized soccer jersey hung on an easel outside the auditorium. The orchestra played and the choir sang. Her diploma was presented to her mother, accompanied by a ten-minute standing ovation from those assembled. All four of the television stations in town sent crews to cover the event. The principal spoke of seeing Emily in the hall on a day when she obviously wasn't feeling well. Smiling as always, she told him it was okay, there were a lot of people in the world who felt a lot worse. With a catch in his voice, the administrator closed his remarks with the words, "Emily is gone. She will never be forgotten."

A joke told to an anxious collection of doctors and nurses by the wounded leader of the free world.

A smile from a brave young woman to calm the people who loved her.

Forgiveness from the cross.

In the Russian Orthodox Church, priests gather the day after Easter to tell jokes. I think there's a reason for that, summed up by G. K. Chesterton: "Satan fell by the force of gravity. Angels can fly because they take themselves so lightly." Indeed, that would explain what they said in the still morning light of that first Easter: "Why do you look for the living among the dead?" (Luke 24:5).

It must have been said with a smile.

Ronald Reagan died on June 5, 2004. In the days that followed, hundreds of thousands of people on two coasts filed past his casket in a show of respect. Most mourners said—and many political observers agreed—that the outpouring was motivated as much by Reagan's life of extraordinary cheerfulness and optimism as it was by his considerable accomplishments. In her eulogy, former British Prime Minister Margaret Thatcher said, "In a time of great distress, he reassured the world that at least one person remained sane. It was grace under pressure."

11

Suffer the Children

An Interview with Kevin Spacey

—⁓—

Now they were bringing even infants to him that he
might touch them; and when the disciples saw it, they
rebuked them. But Jesus called them to him.

Luke 18:15–16

Actors are very busy people, and they are almost always
in a hurry.

Over the years I've had the pleasure of meeting and
interviewing many famous actors. Sarah Jessica Parker,
Keanu Reeves, Charlton Heston, Mary Tyler Moore,
Michael Crawford, and many others have honored me
with their time, although there have been some missed
opportunities. Once, I had the chance to interview an

up-and-coming young comic who was just about to release his first major motion picture. He already had a prominent role on a network television show, but I had a full slate of guests that day and decided not to ask him to join me on the air. The movie was entitled *Ace Ventura, Pet Detective*, and the young man was Jim Carrey. He's not as easy to interview anymore.

Almost all of the actors I've had the chance to visit with are extraordinarily nice people, although there have been some unpleasant experiences. I've chosen to forget most of those or attribute them to the fact that no matter where these very public people go, there is always—and I mean always—someone who wants a piece of them. So they live under layers of handlers and publicists who make it possible for them to have time to breathe.

Kevin Spacey is an Academy Award–winning actor. In fact, I've never seen a movie in which he's given a less than spectacular performance. The motion picture *Seven* is one of the most disturbing films I've ever seen, largely thanks to Spacey's portrayal of the villain. His role in *American Beauty* made that motion picture one of the most talked-about films in years. He was inspirational in *Pay It Forward* and subtle in *L. A. Confidential*. Spacey is a chameleon, taking on the mantle of every character he plays, making the audience forget it is watching an artist at work. He also has a reputation as an intensely private man who does not suffer fools gladly. The television show I was hosting at the time had booked him as a guest, and I had eight minutes to spend on the air with him—hardly the kind of exposure an actor of his caliber needed, even in one of the largest markets in the

United States. Had I been in Spacey's position, I would probably have considered it a waste of my time.

As the show began, Spacey's limousine pulled up behind the building, and the actor headed straight to the waiting area, commonly called the "green room." Since the show was already in progress and Spacey hadn't arrived early enough to visit, the first chance I would have to meet the man would happen in the commercial break immediately before our first segment together. In cases like that, the guest might be as charitable as Ghandi and the host will still be nervous. I was a wreck. On top of this, we had visitors watching the show in the studio that day, including two children. They had the day off from school and were on a field trip with their father. Surprises like that are not popular with guests, and I had no idea how Mr. Spacey would react. Worst of all, word was that Spacey had been asked a rather uncomfortable question earlier in the day, and he was reportedly in a less than hospitable mood.

As the first segment ended, Spacey entered the studio. He carried himself with an air of confidence and pleasant reserve. I introduced myself and shook Spacey's hand, and we sat down quickly to lay a very brief foundation for the interview. It's not the way an interviewer likes to operate, but dealing with a seasoned pro like Spacey can be very reassuring. I knew unless I asked totally ridiculous questions, Spacey would pick up the ball and run with it.

Thankfully, Spacey was a delight. He was accessible, open, and interested. If an interviewer gets those three qualities out of any guest, he counts himself lucky. We talked about his career, his new movie, how he approached his roles, and what might be next. It's amazing how quickly eight minutes can pass when you're working with someone who at least acts like he's glad to be there. He didn't seem to be bothered by the visitors, and we completed the interview and then went to break. Just like that, it was time for the Oscar winner to leave and for the show to move on. But what happened next was what we should have put on television instead.

Spacey's limousine was parked just outside the back door of the building, down the hall from the green room. All Spacey had to do was bolt through a couple of doors and he could be gone. One door happened to be the exit right next to where two of our visitors were seated—the children. Out of the corner of my eye, I watched as Spacey headed toward the exit. It barely registered with me as he hesitated.

I refocused my attention on the camera as the fourth segment began. We were running what's known as a package, a pretaped piece during which I could put my feet up and grab a sip of coffee. I introduced the segment, reached for my mug, and noticed Spacey was still in the studio. We'd heard that he would be in a terrific hurry to make another interview across town, but there he stood—talking to the children.

But it was how he was talking to them that held my attention.

When we are in a conversation, a perceptive observer can tell exactly how deep into that conversation we are. Darting eyes can mean we are looking for an excuse to get away. Impassive, tight lips often belie a lack of em-

95

pathy or interest. Shifting posture can mean discomfort. But when someone really cares, it shows—and it was clear that Spacey really cared about these two boys. He was asking them questions and listening to the answers. He was *engaged*.

We'd had a nice chat, but our interview didn't elicit the genuine smile across Spacey's face now. His eyes were locked into the boys' as I overheard him ask their ages, where they went to school, and whether they liked movies or baseball. I expected him to say good-bye to his new young fans at any second, but in fact, Spacey spent the next two segments talking to the boys, a good fifteen minutes we all knew he didn't have. As he leaned over to hear what they had to say, there was something else that was very apparent—he wasn't speaking to them as a famous Hollywood actor might speak to his admirers. Spacey was spending real time with two kids on their level.

Eventually, the actor smiled and stood to leave. He shook hands with both boys, wished them well in school, and headed out the door. Both boys knew who Spacey was; they'd certainly seen him in the movies or on television at home. It was also clear that both were mightily impressed with the opportunity they'd just enjoyed. But what was even more apparent on their faces was the real joy of having just talked with someone who really, honestly cared about them and who they were. Good actors can make us care about them. Great actors care about the audience. Great people care about individuals. The best people take time for kids.

I don't know everything Spacey and those two boys talked about. I do know I spent more time enjoying what I was watching as opposed to what I was doing. As for our interview, I can't remember much about it; Spacey was gone by the time the show ended. But my sons are still glowing over their brush with fame.

I've tried to imagine what it must have been like the day all those people started crowding around Jesus with their children. Wherever Jesus went, there always seemed to be children present. It was a small boy who brought Jesus the loaves and fishes (John 6:9). Children recognized him and sang his praises (Matt. 21:15). The Bible records his brothers and sisters (Matt. 13:55–56). Jesus apparently came from a very large family and must have been surrounded by children all his life. But on this day, his own followers tried to keep the children away. He was busy and could not be bothered, or so his followers assumed.

Sadly, that's how we all often behave.

I know there've been too many times when my children have needed my attention, only to be shooed away with a wave. Sometimes, harsh words or a stern look has driven them off. As I've gotten older, I've regretted those moments. Ephesians 6:4 reminds us not to provoke our children to wrath, and I've come to believe that short statement carries a lot more weight than most of us realize. Not only are children obliged to honor their fathers and mothers, but I'm also obliged not to treat them with impatience or frustration that might in any way lead them *away from Jesus*. If I show my children—any child—a lesser example of what an adult

97

should be, what kind of lesson does that teach? What kind of parent will they become? What kind of adult? I'm adopted, so I have a whole raft of parents, and my biological mother likes to say that the best reason to be nice to our children is because, one day, they'll be the ones who choose our nursing homes. More than that, Luke 17:2 mentions that those who cause "little ones" to stumble would be better off dropped into the sea with a millstone around their neck. The literal translation of "little ones" refers to children of God in general, but the phrase is close enough for me.

Over the last few years I've become convinced that our primary job as parents is to paint a picture of what God is like for our children. If I'm abrupt, unkind, impatient, and in a hurry, what kind of picture does that provide of the heavenly *Father*? Who in their right mind would want to worship *that*?

It's the kind of thing that will make a dad slow down.

Unless I'm extraordinarily blessed, most of my life is now behind me. I did the math the other day: The date of my birth is now closer to the start of World War I than it is to today. I'm getting really interested in not provoking children to wrath. Kindness, patience, a willing heart, and an open door *are* forms of the discipline and instruction of the Lord that Paul stresses in his letter to the Ephesians. That's a whole lot bigger than simple groundings or no video games for a week.

There are way too many of us who treat children as conveniences or accessories. We operate on the unfortunate presumption that so-called "quality time" equates with whatever time it takes to do what *we* want done. But that is not enough. Bill Cackmis, a leading talent coach who has coached actors and presidents, says "Energy equals investment." Exactly! We say we are providing a future when what our children really need is us. We have great intentions, but what our children have to have is our *attention*—our *undivided* attention.

A big-time Hollywood star took the time. The King of Kings did the same.

How can we do anything less?

12

Hanging Together

Pennsylvania Miners

—◦◦◦—

If I ascend to heaven, thou art there! If I make my bed in
Sheol, thou art there! If I take the wings of the morning
and dwell in the uttermost parts of the sea, even there thy
hand shall lead me, and thy right hand shall hold me.

Psalm 139:8–10

The other day, my youngest son and I discussed our ideas
of heaven and hell. Most parents have that conversation
at one time or another, but Forrest had just returned
from a junior high school church retreat, and the subject was high on his mental list. His group leader at the
gathering had read from the Bible about the lake of fire
and the weeping and wailing and gnashing of teeth.

While Forrest's view of these things is still developing, I've always been of the opinion that heaven is far more than even the words of the Bible can express. Divine inspiration still must be filtered through human vocabulary, and words are frail and insufficient to describe the ultimate glory of God. They are, however, all we have. One of my favorite verses in the Bible is Jeremiah 33:3, in which God tells the prophet, "Call to me and I will answer you, and will tell you great and hidden things you have not known." To me, that's always meant heaven is far bigger, better, and beyond mere pearly gates and streets of gold. I can imagine a lot of fantastic things, and yet God tells me even when I imagine everything, there is still more he can show me. That's a pretty exciting concept when it comes to heaven, and equally frightening when it comes to hell.

Not too long ago, I interviewed a man on death row. John Battaglia's crime made him one of the most despised men in Texas criminal history. His personal history suggested that he hated just about everyone, but the rage he felt for his ex-wife was especially vicious. On a Wednesday night in 2001, Battaglia picked up his two young daughters for their regular visitation. The three went out to dinner, and then Battaglia took the girls back to his loft apartment and called his ex-wife. No one knows for sure whether Faith and Liberty Battaglia noticed the guns their father had arranged on a nearby table until it was too late. Once John Battaglia had his ex-wife on the phone, he used two of those guns to shoot and kill his little girls while their mother listened on the other end of the line. Afterward, Battaglia coolly went downstairs to a local pub for a couple of drinks and then visited a tattoo parlor where he had his daughters' names etched onto his right arm.

The jury needed just nineteen minutes to convict Battaglia of capital murder and slightly more than five hours to sentence him to death. When I talked with him nearly two years later, I found an individual who was scarcely connected to reality.

Battaglia was intelligent, an accountant by trade, but his intelligence was also his prison. He filled the hour we spent together with diversion and blame, self-absorption and rationalizations. He'd deceived himself and bought into a lie. When it came right down to it, Battaglia had lived his entire life for only one thing: himself. It was all about John.

And now that was all he had.

He spun endless justifications for what he'd done, peppered with questions about whether what he'd done was really evil or wrong at all. Battaglia had immersed himself in the writings of various philosophers, but he wasn't looking for answers. He was looking for excuses. As we talked, the twitch of his facial muscles and shaking of his hands betrayed him: No matter how hard he tried, even he wasn't buying the nonsense he was spewing. Finally, about forty minutes into the interview, I asked him where he'd taken Faith and Liberty for dinner the night he'd killed them. He fumbled around for a few minutes and shot me a blank look. He couldn't remember.

"You don't remember where you ate before you killed your little girls?" I asked. And that's when he cracked.

This cocky, unrepentant man was seized with the knowledge of what he'd done. He couldn't evade it. His laughter and selfishness evaporated. His chin began to shake uncontrollably. For the first time since we'd sat down, he was being real. And for a brief moment, John Battaglia turned from the camera and collapsed into sobs.

After Battaglia had been sentenced, his ex-wife read a victim's impact statement to the courtroom and the man who had killed her precious children. Her closing words were an expression of her hope that Battaglia would burn in hell forever. As I sat with him in the interview room of the Palunsky Unit just outside Livingston, Texas, I realized the truth: John Battaglia was already there.

My notion of a perfect hell is to be somewhere so confining that I can't even move my legs or lift my arms. I'm fairly claustrophobic, so even elevators can be unnerving. Add to that a darkness so completely deep, an existence so permanent, and an isolation so removed from the presence of hope that one can scarcely breathe, and I get chills thinking about it. To me, that would create torment along the lines of a lake of fire. That kind of agony would be hell, and I'm not sure I would have done well at the bottom of the Quecreek Mine.

In July of 2002, nine men found themselves in just that position. The Pennsylvania miners were using an incorrect map when they broke through a wall of rock more than two hundred feet underground. The charts showed an abandoned mineshaft one hundred yards away, but in reality, it was immediately next door. When the barrier was breached, sixty million gallons of water exploded through.

The men scrambled to outrace a four-foot high cascade of water, but the torrent moved too fast for them. They managed to get a warning to a second crew of miners even farther below, which saved the lives of their colleagues, but the nine became trapped waist high in bone-chilling water. In total darkness, they waited and prayed while the waters continued to rise. For three days they were entombed as rescuers up above scrambled to save them.

Those on the surface could hear faint tapping sounds coming up from down below, but there were long periods when no tapping could be heard, leading many to believe that the miners had succumbed to hypothermia or drowning. The plan was to drill a rescue shaft down to where the men were believed to be and bring them up to the surface in a basket, but the drill bits kept breaking. It was later learned that had one of those bits not broken early in the rescue operation, it might have gotten through at a time that would have made things infinitely worse. In fact, had that effort punched into the miners' tiny sanctuary, the nine men likely would have drowned right then and there. It was just one miracle among many.

The miners had one very small sandwich between them. The water surrounding them wasn't fit to drink. In total darkness they lashed themselves together, both to share their warmth and so that their bodies would all be found if they died. They wrote good-bye letters to their loved ones. Yet even as they prepared to meet their Maker, they refused to give up hope.

Up above, rescuers pumped pressurized, heated air into the chamber below in hopes of holding the water back while providing some warmth to the trapped men. Eventually, the pilot hole for a rescue shaft finally made it all the way down, and a microphone was lowered 240 feet into the darkness. Only then did everyone know for sure that those who were buried were in fact still alive. From 9 p.m. Wednesday until late Saturday night, much of America held its breath, until a voice from the bowels of perdition was heard to say, "There's nine men ready to get out of here." The country's collective exhale could be heard in every newscast and every sound bite coming out of Somerset, Pennsylvania.

After the soaked and soot-covered men were brought to the surface, only three had to be hospitalized. All were hungry, but in far better condition than anyone predicted. One man admitted fearing that he would never see his wife and children again, but that the slightest chance that he might make it sustained him. Another asked for chewing tobacco, and so many people responded that authorities had to beg people to stop bringing donations of Red Man and Skoal. Still another miner showed the spirit of the group as he winked to the friends who had struggled to save him and said, "What took you guys so long?" Family members prayed and gave thanks, showing the immovable and inspiring strength of mining people everywhere. Mining people like to say they never give up. It was the truth.

In the days after the rescue there was much analysis concerning why the men had actually survived down there. Psychologist, author, lecturer (and friend) Dr. Sylvia Gearing came by our station to talk about the keys to survival and how they applied in this situation. The concepts are not exclusive to Sylvia of course, but she put them better than anyone else I heard on the subject. Survival depends on about eight things: the social support of others; the realization that we can control only what we can; an overall spiritual view of life itself; the ability to focus on other things besides our own problems; the capacity to redefine the situation; optimism at all times; hope in the face of hopelessness; and the resolve and determination to do what must be done to survive. Heroes are sincere, persistent, intuitive, brave, and humble. Attitude is a decision. Entire libraries have been written on the subject. Nine men chose to live it in the dark and cold of that mine.

The word *miracle* was used a lot that day, both in the coal-rich hills of rural Pennsylvania and in the media. And of all the stories that flowed afterward, the most compelling to me was that of miner Robert Pugh. After three days of being sealed in what should have been his grave, Pugh celebrated his rescue by staying up all night to see the sun come up Sunday morning.

There are many words in the Bible that have been translated into the word *hell*. *Quecreek* would do just fine for me.

One of those words in the Bible is *Gehenna*. Gehenna was a real place. It was the Valley of Lamentation, located just southwest of Jerusalem. It was there that resi-

106

dents of the city threw out their trash and dead animals to be burned. If you've ever been to a landfill or dump, you know it's a woefully unpleasant place. Sanitary situations two thousand years ago made those conditions even worse. Combine that in your imagination with a wastewater and sewage treatment plant where nothing gets treated, and add in crematoria and incinerators with fires that never stop burning: The smell, the flies, the maggots, the rot, and—well, you get the idea. Gehenna was not a desirable address. It was as unclean a place as one might ever imagine, and yet Jesus looks *us* in the eye and says we're all headed for much worse if we don't change our ways.

But he wants to dig us out.

Those men who stood in the damp darkness had something important. They were under no illusions, and there was no pretending. The only chance they had was to cling to something bigger than themselves, and it was their only shot. They had each other. They were a family. And family gives us courage and love.

I can understand why one of those men wanted to see Sunday morning. What an appropriate way to celebrate leaving a tomb.

13

Blessings in Abundance

Stephen Cannell and the Willingness to Risk

———⟨∾⟩———

He who sows sparingly will also reap sparingly, and he
who sows bountifully will also reap bountifully. Each one
must do as he has made up his mind, not reluctantly or
under compulsion, for God loves a cheerful giver.

2 Corinthians 9:6–7

Many people whom I've covered or interviewed have
affected me personally. I'm thankful for all of them but
perhaps most grateful for one man who affected my
family.

Stephen J. Cannell is one of the most successful men
in the history of entertainment. Cannell created legendary television shows such as *The Rockford Files* and

The A-Team, plus dozens of others. When the television industry tried to force him into a box, Cannell walked away from it all and began a new career as a novelist. Books such as *The Tin Collectors* and *King Con* became fabulously successful best sellers. Cannell also happens to be my friend, and he even used my name for the principal villain in his book *The Viking Funeral*. Thanks to Stephen, I've achieved some degree of immortality, even if the character who shares my name is a psychopath. Stephen is also what I would call a true man's man. He goes his own way, puts up with absolutely no nonsense, and does it with style and class. He is charming and available to others. He'll take the time to speak with you, and more importantly—*listen*. Stephen also happens to be ruggedly handsome and debonair, and has been married to Marcia, his eighth-grade sweetheart, for more than thirty years. They have three beautiful and talented children, and in Hollywood, Cannell's private success might be his most remarkable story of all.

Most fathers like to see future greatness in their children. I not only plead guilty to the charge, but complete insanity. Both my sons are remarkably talented individuals. Their personalities are fun and exciting and complement each other. Nolan is the future major league pitcher and marine biologist. No one is quite sure what Forrest will wind up being, but either an artist or a minister seem equally possible.

It wasn't always easy. When Forrest was just beginning school, it was obvious that he was having trouble. Certain letters didn't make sense to him, and he simply couldn't write others. As he progressed through elementary school he started to fall farther and farther behind. The staff at his school was helpful, but Forrest's mother and I grew increasingly worried about his progress, and he became more and more conscious of his failures. They were concerned he might have ADHD and suggested that medication might be the solution. His mother and I resisted the idea, and the tests and retests kept on coming. In the meantime, a little boy's self-esteem and confidence were taking a terrible beating, and the phrase "I can't" became a constant refrain.

Stephen J. Cannell has always talked openly about his battle with dyslexia. Most people think of dyslexia as a matter of simply seeing certain words as if they were in a mirror, or reversing letters. It's far more complex than that. In some cases, dyslexia is a lot like color blindness in that some letters or numbers don't register in the brain because the brain isn't wired to see them. In Stephen's case, he once couldn't use a touch-tone phone, because certain numbers were invisible to him. For years, he wrote most of his stories on yellow legal pads because typewriters made no sense to him. The problem went undiagnosed through Stephen's teenage years, and he flunked out of two schools. Nevertheless, Stephen listed his ambition to be an author under his yearbook photograph. Today, he grins and admits that listing that profession was pretty confident for someone who couldn't pass most of his English courses.

Dyslexia need not be a disability, but it is a learning difference. The truth is, we all learn differently. When those differences are identified, teaching techniques can be adjusted to be more effective. But dyslexia is sneaky. It can exist undiscovered, and its results can mimic those produced by ADHD, behavioral, and emotional problems. Imagine being a child and only seeing twenty letters in the alphabet because your mind simply isn't *wired* to see the rest! The frustration over not "getting" what other children seem to handle without any trouble becomes overwhelming and dyslexics can fall into hopelessness. Many parents and doctors reach for the pharmacy, when medication is exactly the wrong thing to do. Some statistics suggest that if dyslexics do not receive help by the fifth grade, dropping out of school or failing out are almost inevitable. Stephen Cannell supports a foundation that's dedicated to teaching people about dyslexia and providing information and support for families who encounter it. Thanks to Stephen and others like him, educators, doctors, parents, and children can be armed with the tools they need to actually make the most of this learning difference. They not only conquer, they *surpass* expectations.

But to give any of us hope, the people who've been through life's challenges have to be willing to share how they overcame them. That often takes a very special person.

We finally got around to the subject of dyslexia the second time I interviewed Stephen. Forrest was in the third grade about then, and the knot in our stomachs was beginning to grow. Stephen talked about how the condition had affected his life and how he'd beaten it. Many dyslexics become true overachievers—people who find ways to succeed almost *because* of the challenges before them. The more we talked, the more we got into the intricacies and subtleties of dyslexia. I listened to what dyslexics have to deal with, and the picture settled somewhere into the back of my mind.

Forrest had survived up through fourth grade thanks to a lot of things. He was blessed to go to a very fine school in a very good school district that was filled with great teachers and administrators who genuinely cared about his success. But now fifth grade was ahead, and then junior high school—and we all knew that if Forrest wasn't properly equipped and confident, sixth grade was bound to chew him up. We knew we were running out of time, and that's when what Stephen had said started to make sense.

We went to his website and followed the links to the Orton Foundation. Specific testing was clearly recommended. A wonderful school nearby in Dallas deals exclusively with youngsters who have a wide spectrum of learning differences, and Forrest's mother set up still another test. But this time, we knew what we might be looking for. Sure enough—Forrest had dyslexia. Not a profound case by any means, but just enough to cause him trouble and make him feel unhappy about himself. With that new information, Forrest immediately began a series of weekend classes specifically designed to help him. The lessons often seemed irrelevant and miserably repetitive, but the things you and I might take for granted can be brick walls for dyslexics. He did a lot of sitting on Mom's lap reading together, but by the end of that summer, we had a miracle on our hands. We had a boy who was ready and eager for fifth grade.

As I write this, Forrest is in junior high school and is having a ball. He's an accomplished artist whose work is already professional in its quality. The grades are good enough, and he's excited about his future. That's a far cry from the little boy who had once been afraid to raise his hand or take a spelling test. He'll always have to deal with his particular learning difference, but he's adjusted to it, and now he knows he can do anything he puts his mind to. He knows he can fly, inspire, or lead.

One weekend, I found myself in San Francisco, driving down the highway with a copy of *The Viking Funeral* on the seat next to me. I picked up the phone, dialed directory assistance in Los Angeles, and got the number for Stephen Cannell's production company. It was the weekend, so I knew I'd have to leave a message.

I got through to Stephen's voice mail and thanked him for making me the bad guy in his book. More importantly, I thanked him for sharing his life story with the rest of the world and for helping to change the future for my son. Stephen called me back that afternoon. I could have thanked him for years and it still wouldn't have been enough. If it hadn't been for Stephen's willingness to be open and honest in yet another interview about who he is, we might never have found out exactly who Forrest is and what he needed.

Stephen J. Cannell will be doing things his way as long as he's on this earth. I can't imagine anyone who commands more respect in his business. I think the *reason* he commands so much respect is because he gives so much of himself—creatively, professionally, and personally. The man knows who he is, remembers where he came from, takes the *time*, and puts his heart into everything he does.

Many lessons have been taught and books written on the subject of giving. We constantly need to be reminded that giving not only enriches the recipient, but perhaps more importantly, the giver (Luke 6:38). But how much greater is that gift when it comes with *risk*? Will people think I am foolish? Will they make fun of me? Will they laugh at me behind my back? What if I open up, not only my wallet, but also my heart? What if I expose my weaknesses? What if I make myself *vulnerable*?

Perhaps no one understood that better than Joseph of Arimathea.

Joseph was of good stock. Born at Arimathea, or "a city of the Jews," his hometown was likely Ramatha, the birthplace of the prophet Samuel. Matthew records that Joseph was wealthy and a disciple of Jesus (Matt. 27:57), while Mark and Luke say he was a member of the Jewish council known as the Sanhedrin (Mark 15:43; Luke 23:50). Joseph was looking for the kingdom of God, and although he personally hadn't participated in the Sanhedrin's condemnation of Jesus, he may have simply avoided being there for the vote (Luke 23:51). Most of us would understand if Joseph merely abstained or failed to make the meeting completely. His discipleship could ruin his career and reputation. Joseph had a lot to lose.

According to Jewish law, Jesus needed to be properly buried before the Sabbath. Joseph was in a position to do something, he had the means to get it done, and he had the credentials to get in front of the people who could give the green light. So Joseph gutted up. The Bible says he took courage (Mark 15:43) and went to Pilate to ask for Jesus's body.

The chance Joseph was taking is almost unimaginable for us, but he knew he could do no less. Joseph told Pilate that Jesus was dead and that he would provide his family's own crypt for interment. Even better, things would be done quickly and with some dignity. Some commentators believe Pilate may have been acting from his own sense of guilt, but for whatever reason, the Roman governor agreed. Joseph, along with his old friend and fellow councilmember Nicodemus, took Jesus's body and headed for the cemetery.

But what if a member of Pilate's staff let the word get out? What if a neighbor saw them on the way? What if someone asked them what was inside those linens, or what all those spices were for? What if all this got back to the Sanhedrin? There would be a lot of uncomfortable explaining to do.

It's hard for people in high positions to open up. Tenderness, forgiveness, kindness, and thoughtfulness—we're often told that those characteristics show weakness and that they should be avoided. We refuse to budge because we're sure a loved one will take advantage of us, a competitor will use these things against us, or our vulnerability will come back to bite us. Forget about giving back. Let someone else do that. We don't want to get burned. We're mindful of the popular phrase, "No good deed goes unpunished." That phrase might even be true sometimes.

But I'd like to be more like my friend Stephen Cannell. I need to be more like Joseph of Arimathea. Either way—I'd wind up looking more like Jesus.

14

Greater Love Hath No Man

Rose's Burgers, a Dallas Tradition

—◦◦◦—

> The accuser of our brethren has been thrown down,
> who accuses them day and night before our God. And
> they have conquered him by the blood of the Lamb and
> by the word of their testimony, for they loved not their
> lives, even unto death.
>
> Revelation 12:10–11

There will never be better hamburgers than the ones
Rose made.

Rose started her little restaurant just off Greenville
Avenue in Dallas, Texas, way back in 1949. I don't think
the place has changed much since then. Every morning
she trundled up to the counter carrying her Tupperware

containers of ingredients. There weren't a lot of different ways Rose made you a burger—double meat, single patty, with cheese or without, and hold the onions was about as far as it went. The building itself was a little run-down red shack of a place, with a ceiling so low that anyone over 6'4" had to stoop in some parts of the main "dining room." The only reason the city health department never shut the place down is because the health department workers all ate there. The floors were uneven and the screen door creaked like an old man's knees. Rose's husband sat outside in a rickety metal chair with an old dog at his feet, and if he didn't like the cut of your cloth, you might not get inside. He passed away several years ago, but the old dog stayed for many more. I don't think I ever saw that animal move, not even when one of a half dozen cats in the vicinity walked right under his big black nose.

There was no cash register. You paid on the honor system. Don Henley, cofounder of the rock & roll group, The Eagles, has a home in Dallas. He values his privacy like no one I've ever seen, but Don was at Rose's all the time. It was the kind of place where you could slip in and out unnoticed. But he is Don Henley, and the inside of his wallet usually looks different than yours or mine. Once, he wanted to pay for a six-dollar burger with a one-hundred-dollar bill—and tried to get Rose to keep the change as a sign of respect. Rose told him she didn't take bills that big, so Henley asked her to just charge his next burger to the bankroll the next time he came in. Instead, Rose suggested Henley leave her his driver's license and run down to the bank where he could break that C-note into smaller bills so he could pay the bill. Henley obliged.

The soft drinks were in the old soda box Rose used since Eisenhower was in the Oval Office. There was no fancy sign out front, just some of those do-it-yourself letters you can buy at the hardware shop. Rose never let her picture get in the newspaper, and for years she asked reporters not to divulge her address. She said she couldn't handle the publicity. There was no parking lot, just an alley and a gravel area where pickup trucks and Porsches pulled in every day, except Sundays. Family members say that in all those six decades, Rose never missed one day of work. The first time a friend took me to Rose's, it looked like we were going to make a drug buy. All I could see was a lonely industrial alley and a dilapidated old shack, inside of which a little old woman barely five feet tall stooped over a 1950s-era stove. She peeked over the top of her thick bifocals and said, "What'll you have, hon?" She never once stopped pressing down the patties onto the stove and flipping them over, not even when she smiled.

And then I had one of Rose's burgers. Just enough beef, with more lettuce and pickles piled on top than I thought you could get between two pieces of bread. No fancy seasoning. Perfectly sliced tomato. Wrapped in restaurant tissue. A bag of chips, and a soft drink. No plate. No silverware. Not even plasticware. Anything you needed was kept in empty margarine tubs sitting on the tables.

I'd picked up the aroma three blocks away, but that was nothing compared to biting into one of these beauties. The juice rolled down my forearm and dripped off my elbow. As I sat among watercolors painted by Rose's nieces and nephews, grandchildren and great-grand-children, the taste exploded into my mouth. The steam from the meat rose toward the eatery's artwork—gathered through years of "free-with-your-next-fill-up" and S&H Green Stamps. I rested my elbows on the Formica tabletop and leaned back in a chair with slightly torn plastic upholstery. It was a perfect combination of beef, fresh fixings, warm bread, and cheese. I've had a lot of great hamburgers over the years, but I have never enjoyed one like that. I imagined eating three but could barely finish the one.

Greek mythology is wrong. They do not serve ambrosia on Olympus. They serve Rose's hamburgers. If I had to choose my last meal, it would be one of Rose's double-meat/double-cheese delights, with Ruffles and a Dr Pepper. Not to slight the many other great burger joints I've known, but a Rose's hamburger was clearly The Mother of All Sandwiches. Do not argue the point, because you'll be wrong. You simply must trust me on this. It was the perfect hole-in-the-wall culinary experience, from the meal itself to the "Welcome Home" sign that hung on the front door. I went to Rose's on some of the best days I've ever had, and intentionally sought it out on a few of the lowest. I've taken friends there after funerals. *Home* is exactly what it was, because Rose not only served great food—she served nourishment for something deeper. It was soul food.

I've seen some stories and events up close. Others I've seen unfold from thousands of miles away. Like most

Americans, my attention was riveted by what was happening on the other side of the world in early 1991.

For months, coalition forces led by the United States had been building up military resources for the attack that would push Iraqi forces out of Kuwait. The news was filled with stories of chemical weapons, Scud missiles, and Saddam Hussein's supposedly fearsome Republican Guard. News-gathering organizations prepared for the inevitable by compiling information on the latest military hardware, creating new maps and graphics to help tell the story, and hiring military experts to analyze what was happening.

At the time, I worked the morning show at a Dallas radio station. My official shift ended around two in the afternoon, but I always stayed late into the afternoon to do some work. The place thrived on creativity and dedication, and no one wanted to leave early. KVIL was just a great place to work. There was a television at my desk, both to keep me informed as to what was going on and to pass the time when the creative juices weren't flowing. Lately, it had become my way of watching for the moment when Operation Desert Shield would take on a new name.

I was watching the *ABC Evening News* with Peter Jennings that afternoon when suddenly the network reporter assigned to Baghdad broke in to report that air raid sirens were sounding in the city and that thundering explosions could be heard in the distance. Night-vision lenses throughout Baghdad captured a scene right out of *Star Wars*, as antiaircraft artillery filled the night in pursuit of the coalition air armada. It was the start of a war unlike any ever seen before. Not only would it be extremely short, it would be extremely quick—featuring the largest tank battle in the history of combat.

It would be a rout, it would be controversial—and every second of it would be seen by the entire world thanks to the presence of reporters, journalists, and cameras on both sides of the battle line.

It's hard to imagine any journalist filing reports from Berlin during the height of World War II, or from Pyongyang during Korea. Reporters did travel behind enemy lines to Hanoi during Vietnam, but they were few and far between and had almost zero access to anything. But for Desert Storm, it seemed there was a western reporter on every corner, a live picture from every roof in Baghdad, and a microphone in front of every coalition soldier. Every day, there were debriefings for the press, featuring something entirely different—cockpit and nose cone views of bombs and missiles hitting their targets; a video of a truck just barely dodging a guided bomb as it slammed into a bridge over an ancient river; the look from the business end of a missile as it sailed through a window and into the laps of some unlucky Iraqis. Hundreds, if not thousands of images, captured our imagination.

Media darlings arose instantly: the calm of Secretary of Defense Dick Cheney; the discipline and dedication of General Colin Powell; the irascible Norman Schwarzkopf, who seemed to have come right out of central casting. It came across as a giant video game with perfect characters. It was also totally misleading to the viewer, because there was real war on the ground and in the air.

121

People were risking their lives and people were dying. Condensing war onto television is an extremely dangerous thing. People who have been through actual war will tell you that it is dirty, filthy, nasty, and indiscriminate. Television makes war seem small and clean, and many people believe it lulls us into thinking war can be surgical and precise. The sterility we saw was a fraud. Most commanders and responsible leaders know that war is anything but sterile or surgical on any level, and they fear that television's "packaging" of war can make it all too easy to get into one.

I remember dashing into the studio to jump on the air with word that Desert Storm was underway. The newsroom gathered its prepared materials, and we went nonstop with coverage for the next six hours. There were overnight updates every fifteen minutes, and most of us thought we would be in what we'd nicknamed "Code Blue" for months. But it was over in what seemed like minutes, not days. The Iraqis cut their losses and surrendered, but Saddam Hussein lived to bedevil another day.

There is so much to remember from those days, but the thing I remember most actually happened before the battle ever began. A television camera crew was traveling with a company of United States Marines. Marines have a well-deserved reputation for toughness and skill. The public image is that Marines don't cry, don't feel, and don't quit. This perception is cultivated and encouraged, because on the battlefield one often doesn't have time to feel. Training and discipline must take over, simply as a matter of survival. In the heat of battle, Marines have time for little else.

The television revealed a Marine colonel talking to his men. They stood at ease among the whirling desert winds, heat, sand fleas, and loneliness while the camera captured what the colonel said:

"What is it that makes a man go into battle? Love. What makes people able to do things they never thought they could do before? It's love. How can people meet challenges they never thought they could overcome? Love. How can a ninety-pound woman lift a car off her injured child? It's love. What makes a man jump on a grenade, costing his own life but saving the lives of his friends? It's love. You don't do it for Mom, apple pie, hot dogs, baseball, Mary Lou in Lost Overshoe, Iowa, and you don't even do it for your country. You do it out of love. You do it for your buddy. You do it for your buddy."

Jesus said that very same thing.

He said, "Greater love has no man than this, that a man lay down his life for his friends" (John 15:13). At first glance, it would appear that Jesus is talking about what we've come to call the "ultimate" sacrifice—literally dying for someone else. But as magnificent or admirable as that might be, it's only part of what the Carpenter means.

We get a sense of this at the Last Supper. It was an evening that began with the King of Kings washing the feet of his followers. He commanded his followers to love each other as he loved them (John 13:34) and told them that others would know who they were by how they treated each other (John 13:35). He asked if Peter was willing to lay down his life (John 13:38) and told them all that the only path to peace was the one he was willing to walk (John 14:6). He promised great things to those who chose that path as well—things that were even better than what the disciples had seen (John 14:12). He told the men at the table that the only way to show their commitment was by walking the walk (John 14:15) and that God would send the Holy Spirit to counsel, comfort, and strengthen them. They would never be alone (John 14:18), and they would have peace (John 14:27). Sometimes things would be hard (John 15:2), but if they kept the faith (John 15:10) they would know true joy (John 15:11).

He told them and us not only to die for each other, but to live for each other: to die to *ourselves*.

That flies in the face of everything we're told. If you're old enough or watch the cable station TV Land, you may remember the old beer commercial that trumpeted, "You only go around once in life, so grab all the gusto you can!" Do we ever. There are corporate executives who loot their companies and betray their stockholders. There are politicians who will stop at nothing to hold onto power. There are manufacturers who cut corners and employees who skim company supplies. They make my newscast every day, but they are far from alone. We steal time from our families and shortchange our spouses. We hold onto our hearts and feed others cold leftovers. We hang onto our lives. We refuse to lay them down.

The soldier on the battlefield gives up his life long before the battle. Most of us will never do anything quite that dramatic, but we have every chance to do something just as valiant. Rose did exactly that, every day except Sunday, for more than sixty years. Her head hung low from a spine curved and bent from a half *century* of standing over a hot stove, flipping burgers. She made every one of her hamburgers with love. Every burger made people happy, and that made Rose happy. It was what Rose loved. Every time I asked her if I could do a story on her, Rose said no. She never wanted fame. She was simply laying down her life. In her words, she only wanted to run her business "one burger at a time." Everything else she laid down.

Rose Stivers died on a Monday morning. It was December 1, 2003. She was two days short of her eighty-ninth birthday. On the giant sympathy card the family posted outside, someone simply wrote "Heaven needed a great hamburger." I'm convinced Peter and Paul are sharing one now.

I can't wait to see you again, Rose. Double meat, with cheese. Just like always.

15

Feed My Sheep

Where Angels Work

—⁂—

Then the righteous will answer him, "Lord, when did we see thee hungry and feed thee, or thirsty and give thee drink?"

Matthew 25:37

Chances are you know an angel.

There are a lot of different ideas and a lot of disagreement about what these creatures are and how they operate.

The word *angel* is traditionally used to describe heavenly beings, a higher order of spirits that exist just above humans in the celestial ranks. There are angels of God and angels of Satan (Matt. 25:41), and Satan was an angel himself (2 Cor. 11:14). But both the Hebrew and Greek words commonly translated as "angel" mean the same thing: *Mal'akh* or *angellos*, they are *messengers*. In some cases, such as Luke 7:24 and James 2:25, the term is applied to human beings. God's messengers.

I often wonder if that man on the corner holding the cardboard sign might be one—just waiting to see what I'm going to do. Even if I don't take Hebrews 13:2 literally—"Do not neglect to show hospitality to strangers, for thereby some have entertained angels unawares"—it's enough to give me pause. But regardless of what you may believe about these beings, I am quite sure there are flesh and blood angels around us every day right here on earth.

One of the best things about my job is that I've met so many of them.

If there's a hospice in your town, angels work there. Where I live, there's a home for children who have AIDS. Being HIV-positive is not the automatic near-term death sentence it used to be, but the epidemic is still enormous, and since a child's immune system isn't well developed, AIDS can be far worse on children. But at Bryan's House, there are men and women who help many of these children by doing something very simple—they hold them.

That's all. They just hold them. Sometimes for hours on end, rocking them back and forth, singing songs to them, and making them feel loved. Many times, it's the only human contact these children will have outside of doctors and nurses. Anyone who has ever held a child in love knows the bond forms very fast. Love is a velvet ribbon that ties hearts together like the strongest steel; it hopes, dreams, wishes, prays, and doesn't just go away. But these angels tie that ribbon knowing all the while the chances are great that they will very soon have to let that child go forever. These people are angels.

Another place in my city where angels work is a foster facility called Jonathan's Place.

A friend of mine named Lisa Matthews started Jonathan's Place more than a decade ago when she took two small children into her own home. The parents of the children were in deep trouble and the little ones needed a place to stay. Even though Lisa had two sons and responsibilities of her own, she opened her heart and her doors. After a while, Lisa and several supporters found an old crack house on the east side of town, completely restored it, and turned it into a haven for even more children. Now fourteen years later, Jonathan's Place is breaking ground on a sprawling campus of cottages where an even greater number of children will be able to find love while their parents face their problems. Not too long ago, I saw two major local charitable groups present checks for more than a million dollars for the construction of the "new" Jonathan's Place. More than one hundred people gathered for the groundbreaking that day, all attracted by an angel named Lisa Matthews.

Anyone from a social worker to an attorney can be an angel. Maybe it's the woman with the sunshiny disposition behind the counter at the nearby coffee shop or the fellow selling papers with a smile at the newsstand. Anyone may qualify. Human angels usually shun the spotlight, feel rather uncomfortable when I call them angels, and don't make a big deal about their angelhood.

People in the public eye are often asked to give a little time and effort to charitable causes. It looks good on the resume, it's a good chance to promote the station where one works, and it's a wonderful way to pay something back to the community. Those are all great reasons, but I've yet to find one reason that trumps the chance to be inspired. Most of us get far more out of the experience than we can ever hope to return.

One year, we were producing a special radio documentary for the holiday season. We wanted to go to unusual places where the spirit of Christmas was perhaps most vividly illustrated. Radio documentaries are more fun than those on television because you don't have the luxury of pictures. The whole story must be conveyed with sound and good writing.

One such story involved the True Love Missionary Baptist Church of Dallas, Texas. Each year, a few days before the holidays, church members spend a Saturday morning gathering food for the needy in the neighborhood. On this side of Dallas, there is a lot of need, and even though the church is far from opulent, it puts aside its own needs to serve others who are even less fortunate. There are burglar bars on most of the windows in that area, and the nearby used car lots are surrounded by fences topped with razor wire. When I got to the church, the back door was wide open. No one was around, so I went inside. The only sound came from the kitchen in the family center where you could hear someone preparing breakfast for the volunteers who would show up later. The smell of scrambled eggs, biscuits, grits, and bacon was incredible. I followed the aroma, carrying my tape recorder and microphone, and met a middle-aged woman with a cast-iron skillet in her hand.

At that point most people would expect at least a little apprehension from the unsuspecting hostess. She didn't even flinch. In fact, she didn't ask who I was, or what I wanted, or what I was there to do. One might have expected her to be at least a little taken aback, but there was none of that. The woman never even looked up, and asked only one question.

"Are you hungry?"

When the first thing a person says to you is "are you hungry?" *that* is a church.

Another piece in the documentary involved a very good friend of mine and one of the finest angels I've ever had the chance to meet: Santa Claus.

Rumor has it that Santa's real name once was Jim Neville, but that was just a cover. As far as I'm concerned, he *is* Santa. His main address is, of course, the North Pole, but Santa and his wife also keep another home in the small town of Krum, Texas. Naturally, Santa has a woodworking shop—and yes, he makes toys there. His car horn even plays "Jingle Bells." I've never seen him when he isn't dressed in full Santa regalia, and even in the hottest summer, the long hair and flowing white beard remain. But he is Santa in more than just appearance.

For years, Santa made annual appearances at a local bakery. Long lines of kids and their parents would wait in the cold for that one chance to crawl up into Santa's sleigh and sit upon his knee. For those children who couldn't attend, Santa would make special trips. There are two main hospitals for children in Dallas-Fort Worth, and each year before Christmas, Santa would visit both.

By the time I got to the hospital in Fort Worth, Santa had already heard from most of the children who'd been waiting for him. "Mall Santas" generally get requests for things like Nintendos and DVDs. But Santa and all of his helpers everywhere know that when you're at a hospital, different questions are going to come. That's why I was there. I didn't know what the tape would capture, but I knew it would probably be good. I snuck in behind the big chair they'd set up for the great man in red, turned on my tape recorder, and started to eavesdrop. There were only about five children left to go. I had to strain to hear what my microphone was recording.

The first child was a young boy of about nine years. For whatever reason, his parents had stopped coming to see him. Maybe it was some kind of custody battle, or despair, or who knows—I never found out. I only heard the request Santa heard. "Santa, I want to see my mom and dad again."

The second boy was even younger. He'd been in a traffic accident. The wreck had killed his father. His request—"Santa, bring my daddy back."

The third child was a little girl who had lost her hair. Her tiny frame was enveloped in tubes and gauze. An IV bottle was fastened to a mast attached to her chair, and the solution inside it snaked its way down a long lifeline into her pale and delicate arm. She had a request for Santa as well.

"Santa, make my cancer go away." Santa kept listening, and the little girl went away smiling.

My friend Santa Claus will tell you up front that he cannot perform miracles. He also won't hesitate to tell you that he knows who can. Santa will tell you and all the children who come to see him that only God can grant wishes like these, but if we pray very hard, sometimes those prayers will be granted. He gets a lot of questions like that, and I can only imagine how much he'd like to personally handle every one of them. The Santa Claus I know is a very big man. In fact, I'll guess that Santa is actually about 6'3" and weighs maybe a little more than 240 pounds. His hands are hard and calloused, yet gentle. His face is lined and weathered, but serene and calming. His voice is booming and unbridled, but it's also soft and filled with laughter. His eyes are bright blue and clear, but that day I saw them brimming with tears. His voice was quavering. I'd never seen Santa *cry*.

Just then, Santa leaned over to me and said something that never made the tape or the documentary I later produced.

"I hope I'm doing some good."

There are a lot of ways to minister. Solomon did it through wisdom. David did it through his poetry. A poor woman did it with two copper coins (Mark 12:42). Anna did it through a lifetime of intense prayer and fasting (Luke 2:36). Zacchaeus did it by giving away half of everything he owned. The sister of Lazarus used a bottle of perfume and her hair (John 12:3). In Latin, to minister literally means to *be less*.

The results are certain. Paul spells it out in 1 Timothy 6:19: It's taking hold of a life that is life indeed.

Jim, if you're reading this—you do the work of Jesus. And I believe in angels.

16

Upon This Rock

Seeing Potential in Others

—✺—

I know whom I have chosen.

John 13:18

My oldest son, Nolan, is a very good pitcher.

I know that every father likes to think highly of his children, and I'm no different. And since I write this while Nolan is in high school, there's no telling whether he will still be a good pitcher in two or three months, let alone two or three years. Arms get tired and other kids get better. Confidence ebbs and flows. Interest and dedication can head right out the door when something more fascinating comes along, whether it's a new calling or a call from the new girl in school.

The thing that makes Nolan a good pitcher is not his arm, although he's been fast enough for the last few years that I won't catch for him anymore (in television, we need our teeth). He also has great movement on his pitches, and my forty-year-old eyes don't pick up the ball like they used to. He has a bunch of off-speed junk he can throw in to trick the batter. But what really makes him or any pitcher very good or even great is disposition: the muscle between the ears. That's what enables them to have the focus to shake off a three-run homer and come right back to strike out the side. If you have a guy like that, you don't just have a pitcher, you have an assassin. You also have a very proud papa.

It's hard to imagine this is the same little boy who used to squall like a banshee whenever it was bedtime. Now, even though he's only in his teens, I'd trust that young man with my life. He makes mistakes, of course—but what's inside him is golden. The same goes for how I feel about his little brother. Their mother has done a tremendous job, and God has blessed me in ways I can't ever count.

It can be difficult for fathers to see the potential in their children early on. As they get taller, things become more obvious. But at the beginning, things like courage, faith, and character aren't so apparent. I think Peter was like that.

No one but Jesus could have possibly imagined anything great about that burly, hot-tempered fisherman. He was originally called Simon, a common Hebrew name—and Peter was a very common man. He seems to have been married (Luke 4:38) and had at least three brothers. Only his sibling Andrew appears to have been able to put up with him. He was a Galilean, a people known for brashness and impetuous behavior. He was rough-edged and temperamental. Paul had to track Peter down and get in his face because Peter started playing favorites (Gal. 2:11–14).

Just from appearances, I doubt many of his contemporaries thought Peter would ever amount to much of anything.

But if there's one characteristic that Peter did possess, it's this: He was *willing*. He would try to walk on water (Matt. 14:29), proclaim Jesus the Messiah (Luke 9:20), promise to die (Luke 22:33), fight when he saw the need (John 18:10), and jump from the boat when he saw his Lord (John 21:7).

There's another man like that around these days, and he's been in the news a lot. I used to watch him jogging every morning, even as I wrote stories detailing his successes and his failures. He was born into a privileged family and spent much of the first part of his life acting like the world owed him an existence. Arrogant and irresponsible, he lived large and partied hard. In business, he was a moderate success, but his first foray into public life was a resounding failure. He worried his parents, worried his wife, and worried his friends. There were times when alcohol got in the way of both life and love. And then one day around the age of forty, this man grew up.

A few years later, someone asked Bush who his hero was. Without hesitation, he answered, "Jesus Christ." There was a lot of snickering over that answer in the next few days, and a lot of speculation that he was simply trying to score a few points with his audience. What many people either failed to notice or didn't take seriously was what he said immediately after his confession—"because he changed my life."

Many people claim Jesus as their hero and yet never say why. Sometimes we drop his name to schmooze a few people, but when there's real evidence of a life that has been changed, the confession carries inestimable weight. Everyone who knew Bush back in his wild days will tell you that his life is truly changed. His confession was guileless, because he really meant it. He has had plenty of opportunities to share the strength he found, in ways he never could have imagined at the time he found it.

I think it must have been that way with Peter too. I don't think Peter really knew who or what he was dealing with until one early morning on the shore of the Sea of Galilee; a man had been executed just days before, one of Peter's dearest friends, and yet there Jesus stood on the land as day began to break. The first time Peter had jumped out of a boat, he sank. This time, nothing could keep him in the boat, and he dove into the water to get to his Lord. But even then, as Jesus made breakfast for the fishermen, there was no way Peter could have imagined the extent of what Jesus meant when he said, "Follow me." We're all like that. We may make the decision to follow, but only God knows where the path is going to go.

That's not to say George W. Bush is Peter. He's not. We *all* are. Of ourselves, we really don't have much potential. The sweaty man I used to watch outdistance his bodyguards on the sidewalk jog at the Ballpark and fumble his way through a press conference was once just as ill-qualified as Peter to lead anything. When George Bush surrendered to Christ, I doubt he envisioned leading a stricken nation in prayer any more than a sopping wet Peter imagined himself as an emissary of Jesus. But both men were lifted above what they were, to become what God needed them to be. We don't choose God. He chooses us (John 15:16). He knows whom he has called. The secret to becoming God's instrument lies in the name Simon itself. In Hebrew, it means *to hear*.

And those who answer in the affirmative are changed.

There's a great old song called "It's Not Where You Start, It's Where You Finish." That's pretty much the sum of all things. I have no idea how history will judge George W. Bush. No one does. No one should deify the man, because a man is all he is—and men have flaws. As a country, we thought we knew everything about George Washington, Thomas Jefferson, Abraham Lincoln, Woodrow Wilson, Franklin Roosevelt, John Kennedy, and so many more. Then we learned more. Some of the things we've learned aren't pretty. A lot of what we know about Peter isn't pretty, either. But we know he heard, and he was willing. You could see the effect of the cross in his life, because he saw everything through the cross.

And it's not really the judgment of *history* that matters. It's the judgment of God.

17

Faith on the Line

Cassie Bernall

—⟨∽⟩—

Now when they heard these things they were enraged,
and they ground their teeth against him.

Acts 7:54

Topping our news tonight, authorities say a man is dead
after he was attacked by an angry mob. Investigators say
it all started when the man, whose name is not being
released until relatives have been notified, interrupted
a meeting of local politicians and religious leaders.
Witnesses say the man made several inflammatory
comments directed at the people in attendance, and
refused to be seated when asked. Several members of
the audience reportedly tried to restrain the man, and

at that point he refused to leave. At this hour, the exact nature of what the man said remains unclear, but detectives say a large number of people then dragged the man into the parking lot. Eyewitnesses do tell us this evening that the victim then shouted something about his religious convictions to the people around him, and at that point, he was attacked. The medical examiner will conduct an autopsy to determine the exact cause of death, but police say the man died of severe multiple blunt force trauma. Investigators also say several bystanders watched as the scene unfolded, but did not intervene—and one individual is said to have shouted encouragement to the crowd, even as he held the jackets and personal belongings of the alleged assailants.

I've often wondered how the modern media might report the stoning of Stephen.

It's not like we don't have similar opportunities. Two missionaries are kidnapped by separatist guerillas in the Philippines, who execute one of the two during a rescue attempt. His wife openly expresses her sorrow but acknowledges her faith in the mystery and justice of God's wisdom—a facet of the story that's quickly edged out by a new crisis. An American journalist is held by an extremist faction and killed because of his nationality and his race. The media's focus quickly turns to the search for those responsible and a debate over whether a videotape of his execution should be broadcast—while the reporter's faith becomes a sidebar. Two young women are captured by forces of an oppressive regime; they pray and sing church songs while being threatened with a potential trial and execution far behind unfriendly lines.

When they are freed they gladly proclaim their willingness to risk imprisonment again in order to teach others
about their beliefs. Their convictions quickly become
fodder for talk shows, where some people condemn
them for trying to impose their religion.

To my dying day, I will always believe that the reason
matters of faith and conviction get relegated to footnote
status has little to do with any organized or palpable
media distaste toward religion. As I've said, there is such
bias out there, but whether there's a greater incidence
of it in journalism than other professions is arguable.
The fact is that most people in our business are simply
uncomfortable trying to tell that side of a story for fear
of being accused of editorializing or proselytizing. The
quicker we can get past the religious aspects and on to
familiar things such as the coroner's report and official
State Department comments, the better. But more than
anything else, I am convinced that some of the most
interesting components of stories today, whether they
are of a religious nature or not, simply get swept aside
by the grinding news cycle.

Much has been written about the changing dynamics
of how we get news these days, but the operative word
is speed. Everything is *much* faster. Before World War I,
parts of America didn't even know we were at war with
the Kaiser until some of her sons and daughters were already at the front. By 1941, radio let millions hear about
Pearl Harbor by the time they got home from church.
Just twenty years later, we were able to watch Jack Ruby
kill Lee Harvey Oswald and watch the Tet Offensive as
these stories actually *happened*. And as if watching his-

tory unfold live isn't enough, these days we have cadres of pundits and analysts who gather daily to predict the future before it happens. One hundred years ago, it took weeks for information to span the continent. Now, events circle the earth in real time. My grandmother was born before we learned to fly and lived long enough to see us walk on the moon. I don't for a second believe she ever imagined watching Neil Armstrong and Buzz Aldrin in space while she sat on her sofa.

Even those of us who've grown up in the television age can't quite grasp it all. In the old days, people got their news by the spoonful. We could chew on it and digest it, because we had time to do it. Now we are overwhelmed by information overload and have to swallow the whole thing at once. Before we can get a grip on what's on our plate, someone brings out a whole new tray. There's zero time to think it over before we have something else to think about, and then something else again. As a result, I think we've developed a bad case of intellectual indigestion. There's no way to get our minds around any issue and sufficiently mull it over with five hundred cable and broadcast news channels blasting us right and left while eighteen gazillion reporters are out there digging for new angles. Add it all up and you will have something new to think about tomorrow before you've been able to assimilate what you had to think about today. Today's facts aren't just marginalized—they are obliterated.

But there are some parts of certain stories that simply defy our insatiable desire for "new." They survive the news cycle, media bias, discomfort in the retelling, or even unfamiliarity with how to tell them. Sometimes, something happens that is just so profound that the story blasts through every barrier.

The story of Cassie Bernall is one of those.

What happened at Columbine High School in Littleton, Colorado, is etched in our collective consciousness. Two troubled loners decided to take out their frustrations on an average school day at the expense of their classmates and teachers, plus anyone else who got in their way. Eric Harris and Dylan Klebold joined that select club of people whose names conjure up images of evil. What they did, why they did it, and how it could have happened are the subject of countless books, stories, and articles. Their behavior is the subject of criminal study, psychological analysis, and legal action. But all that is no different than what happens after any such tragedy. We spend months and years trying to sort it all out, and we should—so we can spot the warning signs next time and maybe intervene before something terrible happens again.

But in the middle of the story, there is Cassie Bernall. For a long time, Cassie had been troubled. There were times when she doubted the necessity of her own existence. She'd searched and, by her own admission, often chose the wrong path. She was rebellious and disobedient, but told people she found the power to change in Jesus.

And at the height of the madness of April 20, 1999, one of the gunmen found Bernall on her knees.

A witness said the gunman mockingly asked, "Do you believe in God?" Bernall chose her convictions. "Yes, I do. And so should you." According to the witness, that's when the shooter pulled the trigger.

The muzzle blast left powder marks on the young girl's skin—indicating the gun was fired at point-blank range. Cassie Bernall reportedly paid for her statement of faith with her life.

Not only was Cassie's story unavoidable, it was critical. It was hard to imagine. Nose to nose with the barrel of a gun, with survival perhaps just one denial away—and yet this young woman chose integrity. Who among us could honestly say that we would do the same thing? Could we confess Jesus as our Lord and Savior if our life depended on it?

Most of us take up faith like a security blanket. In this country, there's little immediate danger that we will ever be threatened or killed. Violent crime does happen, but with 270 million of us to go around, it usually happens to someone else. When it happens, it's supposed to happen to adults who have perhaps opened the door to danger. But to a child who has an entire lifetime to go? To a teenager who has only begun to discover herself? At *school*? Inconceivable.

Defining moments *defy* the moment. Powerful words get around. They echo and reverberate far beyond the horizon. In 1864, Abraham Lincoln asserted that the world would little note nor long remember his words at Gettysburg. He'd followed a speaker who had taken the podium for two hours, and the press ridiculed Lincoln's speech as trivial and meaningless. Defining moments are undeniable. They are not measured by duration, but by impact.

The story of Cassie Bernall's defining moment was later challenged by the accounts of other witnesses. Some maintained it had never happened at all, or actually involved another young woman who survived the Columbine massacre. But most who knew her agreed. To do such a thing was in keeping with who Cassie Bernall had become. Regardless, the story took on a life all its own. A terrified young woman faced with death had apparently opted in a second to do what most of us wrestle with for a lifetime. That was why the story resonated. What would *we* have done?

Many believers tend to think there is only one defining moment: we give our lives to Jesus, and that's that. Somehow, we're supposed to bask in the afterglow enough to do the right thing from there on out. It's a line of thinking that makes no sense. It's like expecting a marriage to survive because the wedding was beautiful. But relationships take work—especially a relationship with God. They can't go on automatic pilot. We must be intentional.

Stories like Cassie Bernall's lead me to believe that *every* choice we face is a defining moment. Who will we be, right now—or rather, *whose* will we be? For Cassie, what may have been her final statement of faith was preceded by a series of life statements just like it—although none of those ever got on the news. Paul talked about training and running the race of life with a purpose. No one wins the race by accident. It takes practice and discipline and intent. The athlete wins because he or she repeatedly does the things necessary to get in a position to win. Cassie's life was not one single defining moment, but a series of defining moments—and she'd come to define herself by choosing Christ over self. When that horrible moment arrived, she *couldn't* have been anything else but his.

Reports of Cassie Bernall's final stand for her Lord were repeated over and over, in spite of the news cycle or any reluctance to "go there." What this young woman had apparently done could not be denied. She had completely surrendered to principle, rather than surrendering her principles. Something mattered more to her than her own life. Even the most jaded denizens of America's newsrooms felt their jaws drop in amazement, and in many cases, admiration. What Cassie Bernall did made no sense. There was no logic to it. It couldn't be explained. Normal people just didn't do that sort of thing. Something else was at work.

God showed himself in many other ways that day in Colorado. Klebold and Harris had carried enough explosives with them into the cafeteria to kill almost all the students in for Lunch A. Most of their handiwork failed to work as planned. They killed thirteen people, but the number could have been much larger. Later, there were enough lawsuits and settlements over the incident to cloud almost everything. The tragedy remains, but the cross stands so large that it cannot be ignored or obscured. It so overwhelms that there is no need to struggle to find it.

Since Columbine, the story of Cassie Bernall has been told and retold in church after church. The report of her example has been repeated before countless youth groups. There are books and websites in her memory and music videos dedicated in her honor. Plenty of reporters and journalists have talked this over among themselves as well. Our conclusions haven't always been the same, but the idea was irresistible in any forum.

The news cycle never had a chance.

18

In the Wilderness

Scott O'Grady

—❧—

Indeed I count everything as loss because of the surpass-
ing worth of knowing Christ Jesus my Lord. For his sake
I have suffered the loss of all things, and count them as
refuse, in order that I may gain Christ.

Philippians 3:8

I remember the first thing I thought of when Scott
O'Grady came home to a hero's welcome: "No one who
loses a multimillion-dollar fighter jet is a hero."

Spoken like a true media type who knows absolutely
nothing of what he's talking about.

I have terribly mixed emotions about being one of
the few people in my family who did not serve in the

military. All I did was register for the draft. One thing I do know is that those of us who have never been in combat or under fire have no idea what war is really like. But that doesn't keep us from occasionally putting our foot in our mouth.

The truth is that unlike the majority of our predecessors in the news business, most people in the media today have never served in the military or been on the battle lines. You might be surprised at how many of us don't know the difference between a soldier, a sailor, and an airman. Most of us also have no concept of what it's like to have someone we've never met or can't even see trying very hard to kill us. It's true that many journalists have been killed pursuing their profession, and the danger to many people in the profession these days can't be overstated. But when someone puts on the uniform of the United States Armed Forces in this day and age, they become an instant target. Being a "hero" begins right there, and that's a hard concept for a lot of us to grasp.

Captain Scott O'Grady was on a peacekeeping mission over the Balkans when someone he'd never met or seen tried to kill him. Flying five miles above the Bosnian countryside, he never saw the surface-to-air missile that blew his F-16 Fighting Falcon in two. With the brilliant orange glow of a fireball exploding behind him, O'Grady managed to grab the ejection handle and punch out. A long parachute ride down to gathering enemy troops is not something I'd ever want to experience, but that's what he faced. That none of the soldiers on the ground was able to shoot O'Grady before he hit ground was in itself a miracle. The minute O'Grady got to earth, they were after him. With only a radio, scant survival supplies, and his training, O'Grady went on automatic: evade and escape.

For six days, O'Grady slept by day and moved by night. Ants were his dinner, and rainwater gathered from leaves, his beverage. Cold enveloped him, and dehydration sapped his strength. The training of an American fighter pilot provides some shield against the hopelessness of any situation because one is drilled to focus on the mission. The strain of knowing that people who want to kill or hurt you are right behind you gets buried underneath that training, but it is there nonetheless, and it eats at the soul.

And every night, O'Grady used his tiny radio to send his SOS into the night, in the fleeting hope that someone friendly might hear it. After his plane had been shot down, Allied aircraft were held to a perimeter over the Adriatic Sea, more than eighty miles away.

For all anyone knew, Captain Scott O'Grady had been incinerated in the fireball that destroyed his jet. The odds that anyone was listening, let alone looking for him, were remote at best.

But late one night, one of O'Grady's squadron buddies decided to make one more turn into the Balkan coast. Defying the odds, the pilot called out to O'Grady in the darkness.

Hearing his radio crackle with a friendly voice, O'Grady sprinted to the highest point of land in the area. From the top of a hill, O'Grady called back, giving his call sign. The wheels of rescue were now in motion.

Back here at home, the news business was riveted by the story of a young American pilot lost in enemy territory. Satellite trucks and live crews camped outside the family home, and military analysts were interviewed about O'Grady's training and chances. The story was about to get even better. At sea, but within range, was an American aircraft carrier, complete with helicopters and Marines. On hearing that O'Grady had been located, the ship's commander immediately ordered a rescue. The helicopters went in, and after several terrible hours of waiting, O'Grady was on board a Pave Low helicopter, bouncing down a Balkan valley while dodging small arms fire from the ground, surrounded by the nineteen-year-old men whom O'Grady says are the real heroes.

There's a lot more to the story, of course. O'Grady's book became a best seller, and his speaking engagements draw thousands. Captain O'Grady never has and never will lay claim to the title "hero." He doesn't want it. But he deserves it, and it has nothing to do with whether he got himself shot down over enemy territory or how he followed the training that helped him survive. It has to do with just three things.

A lot of us in the business covered O'Grady's story, but most of us minimized it, at least internally. A pilot gets shot down on a peacekeeping mission, manages to keep from getting captured, and gets rescued. By the media yardstick, it would have been a much bigger story had O'Grady been captured by the enemy. Images of American prisoners of war paraded in front of cameras have a long and highly rated history: The country hangs on every development, and hopes hang on yellow ribbons. Not having a clue whether O'Grady was alive or what he was going through didn't make great television, although the bells-and-brass welcome home he received made for great red, white, and blue pictures. That might sound cynical, but media people have to think about these things. We look for the grabber shot—the one to send people home with, the one that causes watercooler talk. Television is a business built on images; flags and military bands, family reunions, and tearful but proud warriors are some of the best. To a lot of people in news, especially the younger ones, an F-16 is just a stage prop in the play. It makes for nice graphics and great factoids, but the real juice is that moment when the family hugs their pilot and says "God Bless America."

But what O'Grady said that day before the microphones, and in every public setting since, defied our neat screenplay. The three things O'Grady cites as what got him through aren't the F-16's superior avionics, demonstrated by our military experts. What got him through wasn't the excellent survival training, as reported by our correspondent live from the Department of Defense. What sustained O'Grady wasn't the species of ants documented on Animal Planet or on the History Channel.

O'Grady says he was able to make it because of his faith in God, love of family, and love of country.

Not the airplane, not the discipline, not the training, not the entire armed forces of the United States of America, not good breaks, not bad luck for the bad guys, or anything else even came close. When Scott O'Grady was in the wilderness, it was a deep belief in an almighty, loving Father, an unbreakable bond between hearts, and a home worth dying for and getting back to.

I get to see a lot of people in the wilderness. People who have suffered great loss or tragedy are a staple of almost every newscast. On the one hand, it's heartbreaking. But you may have noticed how often many of them turn to God for sustenance. That's no accident. Frequently, you will hear them say God is the only thing that gets them through the day. I don't think God always wants us in the wilderness, but I do think he can always use it.

For those of us who wrestle with pride, it's another matter entirely. Sometimes we *need* to spend some time in the wilderness.

In Deuteronomy, God tells the Israelites that he led them into the wilderness and let them starve so they would learn not to depend on bread but on "everything that proceeds out of the mouth of the LORD" (Deut. 8:3). As a friend of mine likes to say, it's not how we handle the good times that make us who we are, it's how we handle the bad times. If that's true, then the wilderness can become a *blessing*. I think that's what Paul meant about the ability to be content in all things (Phil. 4:11). What a liberating thought that is.

The desert is God's survival school, but only when viewed through the cross.

Scott O'Grady may have been a hero when he put on the uniform, but the wilderness made him an inspiration.

What a great example. What a story.

19

Peculiar People

How God Can Restore

—⟨∞⟩—

Behold, we call those happy who were steadfast.

James 5:11

There's a photograph on my wall that might be the best one I've ever taken.

For a long time, I've had the habit of taking my old 35mm camera with me out to the little league baseball field. I bought the camera years ago when the space shuttle was coming back from a landing in California on its way home to Cape Canaveral. By today's standards that camera is practically an antique, and when I bought it, I had no idea how to use it. In fact, the settings and manual focus are still mostly a mystery to me. Somewhere in the bowels of unopened boxes there's a very blurry shot of the shuttle *Atlantis* taken at the wrong exposure from too far away. I don't think I picked up that camera again for at least fifteen years.

But when my sons grew older and I became involved in coaching, I decided to pull that old relic of a camera out of the mothballs and have another go at it. I started looking for team pictures, action shots, and the occasional unguarded moment. To act like I knew what I was doing, I occasionally shot black-and-white film just for fun. The truth is, even a total amateur such as I will accidentally get some good pictures shooting a bunch of kids playing ball. But I never dreamed I'd get the picture that hangs on my wall.

It was an absolutely flawless, early spring Saturday morning. My youngest son, Forrest, and his team had just finished playing, and the coach was giving the kids their post-game pep talk. I decided to take a couple of pictures of their tiny huddle when I noticed two people on the other side of the group. One was an adult in jeans, a T-shirt, and a ball cap, standing with his back to me. The other was a young boy, perhaps ten or eleven years of age. The boy was in a wheelchair. The two were playing catch.

The scene struck me and I raised my camera. In the print, the man with his back to me has just tossed the ball up into the air, and his right hand is extended in an underhand follow-through. The small white sphere of the flying baseball is frozen perfectly at its apogee. Waiting on the receiving end is the young man seated in the wheelchair, with both his gloved and bare hand extended in eager anticipation. There is a smile of joy on the boy's face, and though you can't see the expression of the pitcher, I have a pretty good idea what it must have been.

For whatever reason, I've never found those two out at the ball fields again. I'd love to give them a copy of that photograph. I'm not sure I can express what that picture says to me, even now. The moment was rare, loving, hopeful, kind, and a thousand other things.

Most wonderful of all, it was totally unexpected. The unexpected is not the currency in which I usually deal.

Chances are, if you see or read a story about politicians or elected leaders in the news, you *expect* it to be negative. I suppose in many ways that's natural, because human nature almost requires that we eventually tear down those whom we lift up.

The fact is, many of those in authority often do a very good job of tearing themselves down. The laundry list of disappointments is overwhelming: Graft, corruption, indecency, dishonesty, and malfeasance in government officials seem to be the norm, not the exception. I could give you specific examples, but all you need to do is turn on the news tonight and you'll probably get one.

If I told you about a politician who had trouble in his marriage, you probably wouldn't be surprised. Let's say the troubles were so bad that the two eventually split up. "It happens all the time," we reply. Failings are always magnified by the news media, especially when the story concerns someone involved in public life. Fishbowls can be horrible places to live, but we're so accustomed to hearing about these things in excruciating detail that we expect our public servants to fail, and then remain failures. But the truth is, that's not always the whole story. It doesn't always end there.

John Cayce is chief justice of the Court of Appeals, 2nd District of Texas. He and his beautiful wife, Diane, have two daughters and a lively little granddaughter who is as cute as a button. There were the usual struggles early on in John and Diane's marriage. As many couples do, they occasionally fought with each other too. Eventually, the tensions crowded out the romance, and their marriage failed. John and Diane divorced.

That happens to a lot of people, of course, so it's not a surprise when it comes to people in the public eye. Their faults get magnified—often justifiably so—and there is no shelter from the withering light of public scrutiny. Many simply offer some sort of tepid public acknowledgment, pick up, and move on, knowing that soon someone else's personal disaster will replace their own under the microscope. Pick your favorite train wreck, because there are plenty from which to choose. Senators, congressional representatives, speakers of the House—there are scandals of the week all the way from your city council to the nation's capital. Some of these leaders may actually be adroit enough to make the best of their dirty laundry. But even if they move on and recover, the stuff remains hanging on the line, and the stains don't go away.

John and Diane's personal struggle remained largely private at the time, although it was unquestionably painful. They could have left it at that, and no one would have given it a second thought. But they didn't leave it there. John and Diane were separated and divorced for around four years before they remarried.

That is, before they remarried *each other*.

Unlike so many of us, John and Diane worked through their hurt, anger, frustration, and rebellion—and found their love on the other side. Whatever it was that they had before was gone, but it wound up being replaced by something even more beautiful and enduring. Mortal love became mature love. Romantic love grew to complete love. The solution, as John and Diane will happily tell anyone willing to listen, is inviting God to the marriage and not just the wedding.

But as miraculous as even that might seem in our disposable society, John and Diane Cayce didn't stop there, either. Not only did they renew their vows to each other, they now host a seminar in their home church entitled Marriage Reconciliation.

Since that course was initiated several years ago, more than one hundred *other* couples have renewed their vows as well. Just recently, I had the privilege of watching yet another marriage restored while the rest of the current class looked on. A beaming Chief Justice John Cayce presided, while a very proud Diane and one fidgety little granddaughter in a pretty blue dress looked on.

I can't verify it through the archives of newspapers and video morgues of television stations throughout the country, but I have a feeling that sometimes, after the glare of public embarrassment fades, more people than we'll ever know make a positive change in their lives. I'm also quite sure that the majority of these people don't stop with simply improving their own situation: They go on to share whatever hope they've found with *others*. Yes, that's a gut feeling, and I only have anecdotal evidence to back it up.

There's no question a lot of us crawl into shells of arrogance and refuse to change anything at all. Denial and plain old bad habits keep us stuck in our ruts, and though our careers and even our families may survive after a fashion, our hearts simply get harder and harder. Dr. Paul Faulkner says we not only become comfortable in those ruts, but we also go on to hang pictures on the walls and lay new carpet. We make them our home. But I've also seen many cases in which people who have reached a certain state of brokenness take that opportunity to let God raise them above who they have been, and in the process, raise up others. John and Diane Cayce are but two examples of the uncounted and often unreported.

The apostle Paul was a murderer. So was King David, in addition to being a liar and an adulterer. Peter wrote the book on denial and rashness. Mark was so cowardly that he literally tore out of his own clothes to get away from the Roman guard in Gethsemane. Abraham traded his own wife for the hospitality of Pharaoh. In fact, almost all of the great people of the Bible were so completely flawed as human beings that they could not be called great in and of themselves. Yet God took those flaws and revealed himself and his love—and we don't remember them as failures at all. God will reach into our ruts and lift us out. All we have to do is grab his hand.

The Samaritan woman at the well just outside the town of Sychar is actually all of us. She recognized Jesus as a Jew and expected to be treated as a mongrel. Men like Jesus were to accept nothing from one of her people, but here was this tired, dusty man resting at the well, asking *her* for water. Her response was an indictment. "Are you kidding me? I'm a Samaritan. You people don't have anything to do with us. *Remember?*" (John 4:9, paraphrased). She doubts and ridicules him. She argues and quarrels. You can almost imagine Jesus's gentle delight at hearing the woman rhetorically open up the door for what he was about to say. I can see Jesus grinning slightly, saying "Lady, if you only knew who was asking, you would have asked me for a drink of *my* water." What follows is one of the longest continuous one-on-one discussions anywhere in the Bible.

Minutes later, Jesus's disciples return and are stunned to see Jesus talking with not just a woman, but a *Samaritan* as well! By the time Jesus is finished, the woman herself has raced into the city and told everyone about the man by the well. They all come out to see him, and many believe and ask him to stay in their city. If the woman, the people of Sychar, and the disciples didn't know what to make of it all up to that point, imagine how blown away they were when Jesus not only said yes, but then stayed there two whole *days*. And to top it off, the woman completely forgets her original reason for going to the well.

God is constant and unchanging. He is the same today as he was yesterday and will be tomorrow. I used to think God was also the God of surprises, but I'm not so sure about that anymore. God's people and his message are constantly received with surprise, wonder, and amazement—so much so that we often fail to even recognize them. But God is no surprise. Surprise is our *reaction* because we see things from our expectations and not from his point of view. When a mother tells her four-year-old he cannot have another peanut butter cookie, the child is surprised. He might even get angry and quarrelsome. He wants to argue. There's nothing wrong with cookies, but the mother knows too many can make for a tummy ache. Only when that child is old enough to see it from Mom's point of view does he understand. The child who learns to do that without ever having to go *through* a tummy ache is wise indeed. Unfortunately, most of us aren't that smart. Our problem is that most of the time we see things exactly 180 degrees opposite from the way God does. Love those who hate us? Forgive those who do us harm? Lose our life to save it?

It's a most unexpected picture, indeed.

20

A Child Shall Lead Them

Fulfilling a Child's Dying Wish

—❦—

Unless you turn and become like children, you will never enter the kingdom of heaven.

Matthew 18:3

It is rare for a story to move news people to tears on the air. The story of Juan Merlan Jr. did just that.

Early on, Juan's childhood was pretty much like anyone else's. When he was eight, Juan became very sick and didn't get better. In November of 2001, doctors at Children's Medical Center discovered an aggressive cancer in Juan's body. The physicians fought back with dramatic success, and early in 2002 Juan went into remission. But around March or April of that year, the insidious, invading demon returned—and this time it came back with a vengeance. The cancer assaulted his brain and spinal tissue, and doctors knew Juan was going to die. Juan knew it too.

By July, the cancer had spread to Juan's spine, partially paralyzing the young man. Just one week after learning to swim, Juan found himself trapped in a wheelchair. By the first week of August, heavy medication had cost him the ability to talk. But before that happened, Juan had told hospice workers that he had a secret wish.

Many great organizations grant wishes to terminally ill children. Ordinarily, those wishes involve fun things like trips to Disney World or maybe a ride on an airplane. It's hard to say what those things mean to a dying child. By the time hope is almost gone, there's a knowing on their faces that belies their young age. When we cover these stories, we see a look of gratitude and happiness in their eyes that goes way beyond the draining battle they've endured. I can't quite put it into words, but while the face may be pale and stoic, the eyes are moist and bright. It's that look that volunteers take away, and it's what keeps them going when their hearts are broken by the inevitable.

But Juan had no time for Disney World. It wasn't what he wanted anyway. Juan wanted his parents to get married.

These days, a lot of parents aren't married to each other. Many people decide to simply live together, and that's what Maria Montalva and Juan Merlan Sr. had done. They'd been together for fifteen years and had other children. But that wasn't enough for Juan Jr. He wanted to make it official.

Hospital workers and volunteers knew they didn't have much time. People scrambled to find flowers and a cake. Arrangements were made for a Mexican Roman Catholic ceremony, and a priest was called. No detail was overlooked, including a bridal bouquet to match Maria's wedding gown. With doctors predicting that Juan Jr. would not live through the weekend, the hospital chapel was decorated, and family and friends who were able raced to attend. Anyone who has planned even a small wedding knows there is no such thing as a "small" wedding, but even with only a week to get things together and a relatively uncomplicated service, everyone knew that this particular wedding was huge beyond words.

By Friday, everything was ready. Every television station in town showed up, along with reporters from both major local newspapers. Juan Sr. and Maria stood side by side as the priest put God's seal on the last wish of Juan Merlan Jr. Many tears were shed, both by those who witnessed the union and by the bride and groom themselves. Dr. Bob Bash told reporters that the entire event was a celebration of a little boy's hope and joy for his family. Juan Sr. held his son's hand tightly throughout the ceremony, and his voice cracked several times as he repeated his vows in Spanish. Later he told the media that he couldn't believe how many people who didn't even know his son or his family were so caring as to provide such a moment; he thanked God for the hospital, the state of Texas, and the United States. One of the hospital's social workers spoke of how hard it was to encourage Juan's mother, for even though it was Maria's wedding day, everyone knew the doctors' prediction was about to come true. And though he could not speak to reporters with his voice, one had only to see Juan Merlan Jr.'s eyes to get the whole story.

The following Sunday, we reported the follow-up: Juan Merlan Jr. had indeed died over the weekend.

The story ran first on Sunday evening, then again Monday morning, and throughout the day on each of the scheduled newscasts. Television studios are busy places. They are anything but quiet as the floor director, crew, and camera operators scramble to get their shots and turn the anchors to the correct lens. There's always chatter and updates of one sort or another coming from the control room through the tiny earpieces we wear. Newsrooms are even noisier, as stories pour in and editorial decisions are made at a furious pace. Assignment editors work the phones talking to reporters in the field, and police and emergency scanners crackle with the latest dispatches. Two-way radios snarl and squelch with calls from remote units, live trucks, and station helicopters.

The noise ran unabated during every other story. The latest updates from the stock market, new developments from the Middle East, breaking news in the war on terror, and local traffic updates never made a dent—but when the images of Friday's wedding came up on the screen, the people just stopped. Only the machines paid no attention.

"An update on a story we told you about last Friday. Juan Merlan Jr., whose dying wish was to see his parents get married, died this weekend at Children's Medical

Center of Dallas. Hospital workers and volunteers arranged the ceremony for Juan's parents, who have been together for fifteen years. Doctors realized Juan's cancer had spread just last week, and believed Juan would not make it through the weekend. Although most of the cost of the ceremony was donated or picked up by the hospital, a fund has been established at Children's to help pay for Juan's funeral. Juan Merlan Jr. was only nine years old."

Hold on Juan's picture. Fade to black.

There are times in my business when we weary of the repetition. Frankly, we often get as sick of what we have to tell you as you might be disgusted at what you hear from us. It takes a lot to shock or surprise us, because we get used to the idea that just about the time we're sure we can no longer be shocked or surprised—along comes something even worse. A husband whose hate leads him to take deadly vengeance on the wife he once vowed to love forever. A mother compelled by both evil and madness to chase her children through the house to drown them in a bathtub. A woman caught on video beating a small child in the backseat of her sports utility vehicle. A security camera catching a young hoodlum shooting a store clerk over cash that wouldn't support some people for a single day. It goes on and on.

And then one day comes a story of a little boy who understood the difference between death and defeat. We all caught our breath that day. Touching? Yes. Moving? Absolutely.

Sad? Not entirely. Maybe not at all.

I think the reason we all caught our breath over Juan Merlan Jr. is not because of what was lost. It was because of what we learned. We learned, in the crystal clear way only a child can impart, that there can be hope even in times of utter despair. It's the essence of the cross and the resurrection. It's the result of God's love for us. Ralph Wood is a professor of theology and literature at Baylor University. His list of accomplishments is extraordinary, but his honest assessment of the Bible's message is both humble and insightful. According to Wood, the heart of the gospel is that it's always a surprise. It's not expected. We don't see it coming. It comes without invitation and unasked. It's like falling in love. We don't plan it, and we know we don't deserve it. We can't put it into adequate words. When it shows itself—it stops us in our tracks.

Stories about a dead or dying innocent are supposed to be heart wrenching. What's deserved are tears and mourning. The idea that there can be beauty, or joy, or a gift of any kind in such a passing is impossible. But when we contemplate and accept the beauty of the undeserved gift of Jesus, tears and mourning do give way—to an impossible joy.

Children don't require much. They love, they want to be loved, and they want to see those *whom* they love loving each other. Almost everything else is negotiable. Is it any wonder that Juan Merlan Jr. wanted this for his parents?

In the dedication of this book I mention my friend Bob Berry. His wife, Verna, called him Robert, but I called him Bob. There is a reason for this: Few people ever saw Bob Berry when he wasn't thinking of someone else. In fact, I don't know if Bob Berry *ever* thought of only himself. In spite of a lifetime of ill health and occasional heartbreak,

Bob Berry focused on others. There were many times when Verna thought she might lose him, but Verna is the same way. They are considered spiritual parents by a tremendous number of people in their church, and they opened their heart and hearth to countless souls in trouble. I know. I was one of those.

During an especially bad time, Bob wound up in the hospital. Doctors had told Bob at the age of seventeen his body would fail within a year. Now, at the age of sixty-seven it looked like it was failing him for good. Bob was hooked to tubes that fed him vital fluids and medicines, and electrodes that fed data into a spectrum of monitors. Verna, myself, another of their spiritual sons, and two elders of the church were all in the room, checking on his progress. Not long before, God had kicked the slats out from under me, and in desperation I'd turned to Bob and Verna. When no one should have, they welcomed me with open arms and love. I had walked away in favor of self—and fallen far. It was hard to imagine that anyone could accept me back. I'd given everyone plenty of reason *not* to. But between the sounds of the monitors and the prayers at his bedside, Bob had a request of the elders. His breath was short, but his words reduced me to tears.

He looked me in the eyes and said, "I'd like Jody to lead the prayer for me in church. Jody is a great prayer warrior."

Praying with a sincere and contrite heart has always come hard for me. I've tried to negotiate with God, and I've tried fine words to impress the Almighty. I think we all tend to do that, until we have to get real. There are times when we look back and see how our choices

167

reflect how little time we spent in genuine prayer. But as Bob and Verna nursed me through my own disaster, they sensed something that I'm not sure I entirely saw myself. In the midst of his own pain and suffering, Bob's request revealed something he wanted to say to me.

Bob Berry believed in the power of Jesus to change hearts. In spite of how I'd disappointed him in the past, Bob had faith that Jesus had changed my heart.

What allows a man so close to his own mortality the ability to think of others? What creates the unselfish desire of a child to see his family happy? What creates in someone who is sinking fast the desire to lift others up? What gives one the capacity to love unconditionally? It's simple, really. Bob Berry gave up the adult's analytical desire for proof. He had learned to trust Jesus without *reservation*. He became as a *child*. He saw through the eyes of love. When we see people who truly do that, it is *breathtaking*.

That's what little Juan did for his parents, and it's what he did for us that day in the newsroom. It's what he did for anyone who saw his story. He caught our breath away. Like a small boy climbing into his tree house, Juan got to the top two-by-four nailed into the side of the sycamore tree, looked back, held out his hand, and invited us to come up and see. Like an overjoyed climber at the top of Everest, Bob Berry looked back, held out his hand, and invited us to come and celebrate the view together.

It's a clear, unobstructed view of the cross.

21

We Will Go Together

9/11

—⁓—

There is no fear in love, but perfect love casts out fear.

1 John 4:18

The ceremony at the National Cathedral was ending.

For nearly two hours, America's leaders and her wounded had offered prayer and worship to the Lord of the universe. People of great importance stood before the assembled crowd and the nation with tired and reddened eyes, working to stiffen their resolve even as they bent their knees. Pain and shock reigned across the land, even as the fires burned beneath Lower Manhattan and soot blanketed the Pentagon.

In the beauty of the lilies
Christ was born across the sea,
With a glory in His bosom
That transfigures you and me:
As He died to make men holy,
Let us die to make men free,
While God is marching on.

In our studio, the floor director stood motionless between cameras one and two, preparing to signal us that we were on air. Network coverage was concluding just in time for our noon local newscast, and my partner and I would be the next thing the audience would see.

Glory! Glory! Hallelujah!
Glory! Glory! Hallelujah!
Glory! Glory! Hallelujah!
His truth is marching on!

For the first time in almost thirty years of broadcasting, I didn't know if I could go on. I, and everyone else in the studio, was crying. It was different than the day President Reagan had been shot. It was different than the morning I'd been on the air when terrorists blew up the Marine barracks in Beirut, or the day that the *Challenger* exploded. It was completely unprofessional, but I was crying.

The whole country was.

I had been on the air at the radio station the morning it happened. We were just getting ready to do our business report at 7:55, when someone noticed a terrible sight on the studio monitors in the control room.

As our business analyst began to speak, I interrupted him and announced that one of the towers of the World Trade Center was on fire. Instantly, we knew there was no other story to report that day. Within thirty minutes, we knew that the tragedy was an intentional act. Within an hour, we knew that the entire world had changed forever. I remember little else that day, until I walked into my house late that night and collapsed.

I was blessed. There were many people who would never go home again.

The stories began to trickle out at first. Within twenty-four hours, the trickle became a flood.

There was terror, horror, and hopelessness—countered by sacrifice, bravery, and heroism. There were the firefighters and police officers, chaplains and rescue workers who had climbed into the darkness. The last good-bye carried by cell phones. The couples who had argued that morning before work, and now the remaining partner wished they had those moments to live over again. There were the passengers aboard an ordinary morning flight who defied the ordinary over the peaceful hills of Pennsylvania. There were so many stories. So many. Even with the passage of time, the stories have only barely begun to be told.

And there is one story that still gets me every time I hear it. It always will.

There is great disagreement over how many people jumped from the towers. Some witness accounts place the number in the dozens; other estimates put the total at well over two hundred. Many pictures never shown on television or in print reveal scores of people leaning out of windows above the fires. Experts say that when confronted by the agony of perishing by fire or jumping from a burning building, most people will choose to meet destiny on their own terms. Documentary microphones at the scene that day captured the sound of the impacts. Some people tried to shimmy down the outside of the buildings and lost their tenuous grip. Many more opted to just step into eternity. And many of those jumped *together*.

There were couples. In some cases, there were groups. Camera operators and photographers caught some of them in their lenses. One eyewitness account tells of two people above the fire who kissed, embraced, held hands, and met death together.

Some might suggest that these people were dead already—lost in a hopeless situation. But even when things are hopeless, most of us tend to fight with hammer and tongs. Most of us scratch and claw for the last shred of life available to us in every way we possibly can. Self-preservation is maybe our most powerful instinct. Self-absorption is perhaps our most powerful temptation. Surrendering self is not normal. But most of us have never been trapped above a fire in a burning skyscraper. I've talked with people who've survived similar hopeless situations, from plane crashes to war to tornadoes. They all tell me the same thing. There is no other moment in which one is more consumed with self, and no time when thinking of others is more *necessary*. Few people actually do that, even under far less stressful circumstances. Few hold hands. I cannot even conceive what must have gone through the minds and hearts of those who were trapped. But God knows.

And he was there on 9/11.

It's perfectly reasonable to be in a situation of terror, panic, and hopelessness, and think only of oneself. It's something else entirely to have the presence of mind to think of others. Actually, I think it has less to do with presence of mind than with the presence of God.

The old saying is that no one deserves to die alone. Many of us wish our family members to be with us at the end, and we are gratified when we hear of the dying who passed away softly with their loved ones at their side. Perhaps death itself is not as frightening as is the idea of facing it alone. Any of us who have ever sat with a friend or a loved one in his or her final hours knows how appreciated just *being there* can be. It is not a pleasant experience, but we are there alongside in order to help in whatever way we can. We offer comfort. Indeed, many times in the Gospel of John, the Greek word *parakletos* is used to describe the Holy Spirit. The word is from the verb *parakaleo*, which means to exhort, to encourage—and most of all, to comfort. The only other place *parakletos* in used in the entire New Testament is in 1 John 2:1, where it is used to describe Christ himself. Exhortation, encouragement, and the decision to offer comfort in the face of pain are conscious, loving choices. They are God's deliberate attempt to be with us. Above the fires on 9/11/01, people made conscious, loving decisions not to let others suffer or meet death alone.

"If you will take my hand, we will go together."

Maybe these exact words were never spoken. But they were lived. We don't know all their names; still, let us all think of those floors as filled with hand-holders. I believe they were.

From the time we are born, there are people who have held our hands. Parents, teachers, coaches, mentors, wives, husbands, and many others say to us, "You are not alone. If you will take my hand, we will go together." Over all, there is Jesus Christ—the ultimate hand-holder. A man of incredibly humble beginnings who lived faithfully. Just like us, he knew love, and joy, and sorrow, and anguish, and rejection, and betrayal, and loneliness. But when others turn away in fear, Jesus says, "I am here. I am with you. Take my hand, and we will go together."

Not long before that awful day in September of 2001, I had the chance to stand on the old wooden bridge at Concord, Massachusetts, where Colonial militia opened fire on an advancing British column, igniting the Revolutionary War over two hundred years ago. It was a beautiful Sunday morning in early autumn. Only a few other visitors were in the park. The sun was grazing the tops of the trees as the dew gently glistened beneath the morning mists. From the obelisk at one end of the structure to the famed figure of the minuteman at the other, I was overwhelmed by a conviction that has stayed with me to this day. I was wondering how it must have felt to stand on that bridge so long ago, and how precious it would be to have that feeling in our hearts to this day, and then I realized—our paths are all linked. Our past is connected to our future. The tests are still with us.

Those who gave for us are joined with those to whom we shall give, by *us*.

I became even more deeply convinced of this two weeks later when the towers fell, and when I later stood at Ground Zero.

We *all* stand on that bridge.

Someone held our hand. Someone holds it now. Whose hand will we hold?

22

The Wings of the Wind

Space Shuttle Columbia *Breakup*

—◈—

In their lives and in their death they were not divided;
they were swifter than eagles, they were stronger than
lions.

2 Samuel 1:23 AMP

It was an exceptionally beautiful morning.

Even in Texas, the first days of February are frequently
more winter than spring. It's not uncommon for a final
gale of snow or ice to unfurl during the transition from
the month of January to the next. It's the time of the
Great Southwestern Exposition and Livestock Show,
known to locals as the Fort Worth Stock Show. So often
does winter level one final blast during the event that

176

such weather has become commonly known as "Stock Show Weather."

But not on this day.

A peek through the miniblinds revealed a riveting blue sky. The visible exhaust of a passing car betrayed a morning chill in the air, but there wasn't a cloud in the sky. It was a Saturday. I was up early, planning to meet a friend for breakfast in Dallas. It was barely eight o'clock, and the appointment wasn't until nine thirty. Plenty of time to throw on a shirt, some jeans, and a ball cap, and maybe even stop for a cup of Starbucks on the way. I'd been meaning to go have breakfast with him for some time. Ole Anthony is a self-taught theologian—a man who values his relationship with God above all else—and he has taught me much about both God's love and will. He feels called to the ministry of accountability, and as such, he has made many people uncomfortable. It is a difficult walk, but Ole is perhaps the most humble man I have ever met. I had put off going to see him many times, and I was genuinely looking forward to spending some real time with him. I sat on the sofa to lace up my tennis shoes and absentmindedly clicked on the television to catch the morning news. It was now just a few minutes after eight in the morning.

The morning news program was in the middle of a pet adoption segment, where they bring in dogs and cats from the local shelter and ask viewers to take the animals into their homes. I noticed that the two anchors seemed to be somewhat distracted, as if they were listening intently to their producer through their earpieces, but thought nothing of it. As I stood to go splash on some cologne, I heard one of the two men reference the shuttle landing. I had to think a moment before it occurred to me that they were talking about *Columbia*—and that she was due home today from a sixteen-day mission in space. Shuttle landings take the craft over Texas. Only then did it dawn on me that since the sun was just now into the sky, *Columbia* might have been easily visible in the dawn. They'd had a cameraman up on their roof to catch the shuttle as she crossed the sky. And then they showed the video.

What should have been a narrow streak of light was not narrow at all. It was nebulous and indistinct. It seemed to flare and fall apart. It was all wrong. Mission control had lost contact, the anchors said. Seventeen years after the fact, I could still remember the terrible sensation in my gut as I watched *Challenger* disintegrate in a mighty cloud of orange and white. I grew up with America's space program, as did my generation. When part of it dies, so does part of us—and it had happened again.

I picked up the phone and called the station to see if they needed me to come in—but I already knew the answer. As quickly as I could, I stripped off the jeans and golf shirt and threw on a suit and tie. I grabbed the electric razor, and in fifteen minutes, I was at the station.

Unlike some stations, ours does not carry a Saturday morning newscast, so the newsroom was lightly staffed. The Saturday morning assignments editor who had taken my frantic call was now busily answering the frantic calls from hundreds of viewers who had either seen the light show directly above their heads or heard the terrible booms. Mixed in were calls from reporters and camera operators in the field. Most were just starting their day, anticipating some relaxation with their loved ones, or alone on a jogging trail. Some had heard the story on the news; some had seen it themselves—but all were calling to see where they needed to go. *Columbia*'s trajectory had taken her from the northwest to the southeast, and the desk was getting calls from people reporting what sounded like enormous sonic blasts and possible debris falling from the sky in a general area from south of Dallas to east Texas. I'd jumped on the desk to help answer the phones, and someone produced an atlas of Texas. Quickly, we plotted the reports with a red felt marker, and soon the reports had defined what looked most like a severe storm warning box, stretching to the Piney Woods and the Louisiana border. The reporters and camera crews were told to head that way.

The network had taken air, which meant our station had joined in the wall-to-wall coverage of what was obviously a national catastrophe. Contact with the shuttle had been lost more than an hour earlier, and the clock was ticking. Anything a reporter, anchor, or journalist says without confirmation is merely speculation. As so often is the case, we could not say what everyone already knew: At an altitude of nearly forty miles, at a speed around eighteen times that of sound, in a blaze of superheated plasma, and only sixteen minutes from the safety of home, *Columbia* was gone—and so were the seven brave astronauts she carried.

179

The news director and assistant news director, executive and associate producers, camera operators, technicians, equipment operators, art and creative services personnel, and other anchors were now streaming into the station. When our beepers go off, all personal feelings and obligations must be put aside. Everyone comes in, and some people head out into the field—often for days. Each of us carries a "go-bag" filled with a few changes of clothes, toiletries, notebooks, maybe a bottle of water or two, and a few snack bars just in case. In winter, you want to make sure you have a warm coat and some extra socks, because you really don't know when you might get home again. Even if most of your work is at the station, you always make sure there are a few laundered shirts and some extra ties in your desk—just in case. Of course, today, I had none of that. I'd taken my go-bag out of my truck and showed up dressed in a suit and tie for the anchor desk. That was not where I would spend the day.

Rob Allman, our assistant news director, spotted me at the assignments desk. The assignments desk is essentially the nerve center of any newsroom—a place where split-second decisions are made as to what is newsworthy and how to cover whatever passes that test. I was merely answering the phones. We appreciate calls from the public more than anyone might ever guess. It is very rare that our people or cameras will actually be in the right place when a story of great importance breaks. It's a little like catching a lightning strike in a photograph. So on many stories, ordinary people and eyewitnesses are not only our best, but often our only resource. Rob pulled over someone better able to handle the phones, looked straight at me, and said only three words: "Can you fly?"

Within minutes I was speeding to the municipal airport where the station's news helicopter was waiting. In thirty minutes, the pilot, our cameraman, and I were lifting off into the azure skies of an early February morning, heading toward the debris fields in East Texas. We flew as fast as we could go.

At 150 miles an hour, it took us about forty-five minutes before we were in the area where it was thought *Columbia* might have come down. Witnesses on the ground had been calling everyone from local television and radio stations to the networks, reporting showers of debris all the way from the Red River to Louisiana. It was apparent from the first video footage shot by John Pronk at WFAA-TV in Dallas that the shuttle had broken into fragments, and reports from eyewitnesses suggested some of those pieces might be quite small. We didn't really know what to expect or what to look for, but we imagined that some of the shuttle fragments might be quite hot from the orbiter's reentry, even though they might have cooled significantly after falling almost two hundred thousand feet through the atmosphere. Sam, our pilot, was a tall, lanky East Texan who flew firefighting missions for the National Forest Service. The three of us quickly decided that we would look for smoke plumes from fires that might have been started by hot debris—but we were completely unprepared for what we saw when our chopper crested a ridge about one hundred miles southeast of Dallas.

The horizon before us was dotted with hundreds of smoke plumes.

Many of the plumes were coming from piles of cleared brush, but on closer inspection, as many more were coming from curious patches of browned fields. When the shuttle fell from the sky, it created what was almost a splash and splatter pattern on the terrain. Whatever had started the small fires had come to the ground at a steep angle. In some cases, there were small craters. In others, an odd patchwork of skid marks and ricochets—as if whatever had hit had disintegrated, causing dozens of still smaller swatches of charring and grass fires. More often than not, farmers, ranchers, and residents of the area stood near the swatches, trying to put the small fires out—and trying to grasp what had suddenly started them.

Something else caught our eyes. Many times, folks who live in rural areas use their back fence lines as dumping grounds. In what a lot of us know as the "back forty," we saw scrap and refuse of every possible description, from corrugated sheet metal to junk automobiles. It was everywhere. Some of the pieces were quite small, and they all glistened as we flew over in the midmorning sun. Those who searched for *Columbia's* debris would have to sift through a haystack of junk for perhaps a single needle. Not only would they have to wander through the tangled thickets and forests of East Texas, they would also have to examine just about everything they came across—just in case.

In 1988, Pan Am Flight 103 went down over Lockerbie, Scotland. A team of several hundred searchers combed hundreds of square miles of countryside looking for clues. Those searchers ultimately found the deciding evidence that a terrorist's bomb had killed 270 people—a piece of electronics no larger than a human fingernail. By the same token, a space shuttle is the most complex machine ever constructed, far more complicated even than the 747 jumbo jet destroyed over Lockerbie. *Columbia* had millions of working parts, any one of which might have been responsible for its fiery destruction. How anyone could ever hope to find what might be the critical clue—which might easily be smaller than a dime—boggled our minds. But we had no time to look in detail. We circled, shot as many pictures as we could, and moved on.

As we dropped down for closer looks, we saw other things, some of which we did not put on television. Other crews sent back pictures of a torn mission patch and a charred helmet. The search for the seven people who had been aboard *Columbia* was covered with as much dignity as possible. By necessity, the recovery effort was immediate and intense. There were the families to consider—not to mention the vital information autopsies and lab tests might provide as to how and when the astronauts died. By nightfall, the remains might be forever lost to wildlife. It wasn't long before images of searchers carrying yellow plastic bags were being fed into newsrooms around the country.

In our case, we were too far away for our helicopter's microwave link to carry our signal back to our home base. Whatever tape we shot would have to be physically carried either to a satellite truck with a longer range or couriered to an affiliate station where it could be sent through fiber-optic phone lines. We arranged to meet another crew from our station at a small airport just outside Palestine—just as the Federal Aviation Administration placed a temporary flight restriction over East Texas. We'd just managed to get out of Nacadoches before the flight restriction descended, and now the FAA was expanding it. Even as we handed over our tapes to the airport operations desk at the tiny airport for safekeeping, satellites high above the earth were being reoriented to scan the debris zone and F-16 fighter jets were patrolling the area to clear away the dozens of news helicopters that had converged on the search area. Within minutes, Palestine would also be under the flight restriction and nothing would be able to take off from the airport. Anything that couldn't stay above the minimum three-thousand-foot restriction would have to set down immediately and stay there, probably for several days. News directors take a dim view of having their station's helicopter trapped one hundred miles from home, so we dashed for our chopper to head out while we still could. There was an F-16 in our area; although we couldn't see him, we could hear the roar of his engine in the distance.

The enormity of the *Columbia* disaster was obvious to everyone covering the story. Our first responsibility was to report the story as best we could. Once that job is done the primary task becomes getting back to the station. As we scooted along across the treetops, the three of us were feeling pretty satisfied about having gotten some good footage—and about having gotten out of the no-fly zone while we still could. But we hadn't gone more than ten miles from the airfield before the three of us heard a strange, high-pitched noise in our headsets. It clearly wasn't static, since it cycled and repeated at fast, regular intervals. Very calmly, Sam spoke into his headset microphone.

"We've just been painted."

It took a second before I realized what he meant, but I asked anyway.

"Does that mean what I think it does?"

"Sure does," Sam replied. "That F-16 we heard back there just switched on his targeting radar, and he's locked on us. We're lit up."

Ordinarily, when a fighter pilot wants someone to land, his last resort before opening fire is to "thump" the offending aircraft. The pilot pulls his aircraft above his target, tilts his nose up, and kicks his afterburner. The resulting thrust "thumps" the aircraft below with a very strong wallop. A firm enough thump can send a fixed-wing aircraft with an average pilot into a spin. For a helicopter in a no-fly zone, the operator gets one warning before the fighter pilot does whatever is necessary—and this was our one warning.

Very calmly, Sam keyed his microphone again. "I guess he just wants to make sure that we know he wants us to go home." We didn't have to be told twice. We were there to cover a story—not become one.

I vividly remember the stunned surprise I felt as a boy after fire destroyed *Apollo 1*. The names White, Grissom, and Chaffee were branded onto every American heart—but especially young American hearts that had hung on every bit of news from the space race. Even more compelling was the loss of the *Challenger*. Most Americans understood the inherent dangers of human space flight, but the thrill of adventure and the manifest destiny of the cosmos beckoned. A generation that had been nursed on the heroics of the Mercury Seven had been weaned on Tranquility Base, and fed on *Star Trek*, *Star Wars*, and *2001: A Space Odyssey*. Many things were possible, but not the loss of seven brave astronauts mere seconds into the brilliant Florida sky, and certainly not because America's vaunted space program had cut corners. To this day, the memory of *Challenger*'s fireball still conjures an awful feeling in my stomach. It just wasn't supposed to happen, but it did—and the shock has lingered for years.

Columbia was different. As a culture, we'd become so used to information overload. Maybe it was because 9/11 had ramped up our sense of risk, creating a near-expectation of eventual catastrophe. One war was in progress, and another was looming. The economy was fragile. People were losing their jobs, their nest eggs, and their futures. Great business institutions that had been built on crumbling foundations of deceit had fallen—taking fortunes and credibility along with them. Bubbles of wealth had burst, wiping out many empires built in the halcyon early days of the Internet age. The phrase "shock and awe" was yet to come, but we were unwittingly familiar with it—perhaps especially in the news business.

Think of it. These days we all joke about the "law of three." If two famous people die, we all know that they die in *threes*, so we wait for the next inevitable demise. We allow ourselves to become anesthetized. Even as we scrambled our resources over seven more courageous heroes, we'd been numbed. The thought of yet another symbol of American sufficiency and superiority crashing to earth seemed almost predictable. The hollow, thunderstruck feeling of loss came—but it didn't stay long. It couldn't. Something else was bound to come, and we had no time to waste. Mourning is yesterday, and dread needs feeding.

The families, of course, felt something else entirely. But the rest of the country, and perhaps the world, moved on quickly. Too quickly, perhaps. The astronauts had been so excruciatingly close to home and safety, but even that bit of poignancy dwindled soon enough. There were other crises to address and other stories to cover. We had been shocked and awed beyond our capacity for either—and we all knew tomorrow would bring still more.

In the weeks and months to come, investigations revealed that the disaster could have been prevented. Tests conducted in early June fired a two-pound chunk of insulating foam at a mock-up of a shuttle wing. It struck the leading edge of the familiar delta shape at a relative speed of 500 mph, roughly the same speed at which an actual piece of detached foam from *Columbia*'s liquid fuel tank had struck her wing during launch. The object in the test caused a tiny fissure in the heat-resistant tiles that are painstakingly glued to each shuttle's surfaces. That was all it would have taken. Traveling back to Earth at eight times the speed of sound, *Columbia* had a chink in its armor. The tremendous pressures and fury of re-entry would have created a jet of superheated plasma, piercing the wing and enlarging the wound until a gas blowtorch melted the aluminum infrastructure inside the wing itself. As what happened began to unfold, it was even theorized that a rescue mission could have been sent up to retrieve the *Columbia* astronauts—had anyone known the extent of the damage or its potential.

As with the investigations into the deadly fire aboard *Apollo 1* and the destruction of the shuttle *Challenger*, the scrutiny revealed a number of human factors that contributed to *Columbia's* incineration. A corporate culture protected the danger rather than illuminating a solution. Indeed, human error, oversights, and ego were unfortunate but predictably familiar. But the irony remained. A rather insignificant and lightweight piece of nothing—no heavier than an average package of hamburger meat from your local grocery store—had brought down the most complex machine ever built. Just as it often is with people, *Columbia* was essentially destroyed from within.

The findings had no effect on the profound faith statements of those who were lost, or their families.

Mission Specialist Kalpana Chawla was a native of India who had studied in part at a north Texas university and had logged nearly four hundred hours of spaceflight. Dr. David Brown was a naval aviator, making his first trip into space. So, too, was Navy Commander Willie McCool, who was also a former test pilot. Colonel Ilan Ramon flew fighter jets for the Israeli Air Force, fought in the Yom Kippur War, and was the father of four children. U.S. Air Force Lieutenant Colonel Michael

Anderson had taught other pilots, served as a tactical officer, and logged more than two hundred hours above the outer limits of the stratosphere. Dr. Laurel Clark was a commander in the U.S. Navy and was venturing into space for the first time. Along with Chawla, Clark was also a mother. She had taken special notice from one of *Columbia's* many scientific experiments. Observing a silkworm cocoon that had hatched during this mission STS-107, Clark watched the tiny moth as its new, crumpled wings engorged with blood and flexed. As Clark would tell a reporter, "Life continues in lots of places, and life is a magical thing."

Finally, there was Mission Commander Rick Husband. Husband had wanted to be an astronaut from the age of four, but it took four attempts before his application was finally accepted. His professional qualifications were impeccable, but those who knew him suggest that it was his personal character that set Husband apart. Husband and Anderson attended the same church in a Houston suburb, where Husband sang in the choir. Singing had always been one of Husband's passions, and he used his gift for God. He led a prayer group for fathers in the congregation, but his quiet devotion extended well beyond the walls of the place where he worshiped. In later stories, it was revealed that shortly before *Columbia's* launch, Husband gathered the crew and launch workers to offer a prayer for their safety and success. Many NASA workers later said that of the many things they'd witnessed over the years, they had never seen any commander stop to pray publicly with his crew. Just before ignition, a NASA controller mentioned what a magnificent launch day it had turned out to be. Into his comlink, Commander Husband replied, "The Lord has given us a beautiful day."

By tradition, the astronauts' favorite songs are chosen to wake up NASA flight crews for each new day's work. Husband's wife, Evelyn, chose the one for Rick—a song written by Steve Hindalong and Marc Byrd entitled, "God of Wonders."

> Lord of all creation,
> Of water, earth, and sky.
> The heavens are Your tabernacle.
> Glory to the Lord on high!
>
> God of wonders beyond our galaxy,
> You are holy, holy!
> The universe declares Your majesty!
> You are holy, holy!

Before leaving on STS-107, Husband also recorded thirty-four separate videos for his two children—one for each child, and one for each of the seventeen days the mission was scheduled to last. They were devotionals. Each member of the astronaut corps is required to sign many papers and releases prior to each mission, in case of misfortune. Evelyn Husband would later show Rick's papers to the couple's minister. At the bottom of the final page, Husband had left a small handwritten note especially for the senior pastor at Grace Community Church, Steve Riggle.

It read, "Tell them about Jesus. He means everything to me."

And there was one other thing. Before the mission, both Anderson and Husband had recorded videos to be played before the congregation. In one, Lt. Col. Anderson spoke of the challenges they'd faced, saying, "Rick and I feel we've been put on this mission for a reason, and we've tried to answer those challenges with prayer." In the other, Commander Husband smiled and offered, "If I ended up at the end of my life having been an astronaut, but had to sacrifice my family or live in a way that didn't glorify God, then I would look back on it with great regret."

And then the young father who had struggled nearly forty years to achieve his ultimate dream added one thing more.

"Having become an astronaut would not really have mattered all that much."

Whenever Husband would sign his name, he would add a postscript. Beneath his signature, he would scrawl in the hurried but bold calligraphy of a Navy aviator, *"Proverbs 3:5–6."*

> Trust God from the bottom of your heart; don't try to figure out everything on your own. Listen for God's voice in everything you do, everywhere you go; he's the one who will keep you on track (Message).

On the evening of February 1, the nation and many parts of the world stopped for a few minutes as the president of the United States delivered an address. In part, he said,

> In the skies today we saw destruction and tragedy. Yet farther than we can see there is comfort and hope. In

the words of the prophet Isaiah, "Lift your eyes and look to the heavens. Who created all these? He who brings out the starry hosts one by one and calls them each by name. Because of his great power and mighty strength, not one of them is missing." The same Creator who names the stars also knows the names of the seven souls we mourn today. The crew of the shuttle *Columbia* did not return safely to Earth; yet we can pray that all are safely home.

This same God also sees tiny new moths. As Laurel Clark observed, life is magical—and he is its author. When our wings are crumpled, he restores them. How the crumpled wings of America's space program emerge from its cocoon remains to be seen. It may take a while. But in the days after one terrible winter's morning in the year 2003, God shined through the darkness and spread the shriveled wings of our faith through the lives and commitment of seven brave adventurers, including a humble husband, father, and choir member whose trust compelled him to believe that one day, he would be safely home.

23

With All Their Heart

David Bloom and the Ambush
of 507th Maintenance Company

—◊◊◊—

Fear not, stand firm, and see the salvation of the LORD.

Exodus 14:13

It was a desert sandstorm the likes of which few people had ever seen.

Across the Arab world, many called the storm the worst in one hundred years. The American and British forces had been poised to invade Iraq, but now boiling clouds of talcum-fine dust and hurricane-force winds had nullified the technological advantages of the Allies. Back home, legions of armchair experts were forecasting doom and defeat, predicting with

193

all confidence that the invasion was a failure before it had even begun. Across the frontier, American GIs and British Tommies hunkered down inside of whatever protection they could muster, but there was no protecting against the dust. It got into everything. Smart reporters embedded with the troops had thought ahead and packed small bottles of saline solution to squirt into their noses to keep their sinuses from completely clogging. Soldiers labored furiously to shield their equipment and grab a few minutes of sleep against the gale howling outside each Humvee and tent. But it was a losing battle. No one was going anywhere—to top it all off, it started to rain. Not just a light rain, but a drenching, drowning rain. The invasion had been stopped in its tracks.

Then the weather cleared. And the story goes that when a Marine unit—one of those bogged down the worst—emerged from their shelters and tents, they looked across the ground they'd been ordered to cross. For as far as they could see, thousands of antiarmor and antipersonnel mines lay glistening in the sun. The wind had blown away the sand that had covered them, and the rain had washed them off.

The war in Iraq produced many such stories.

A young man sat upon an armored personnel carrier. It was a strange-looking gizmo, meant for combat but not for battle. It was his machine. He'd designed it, and it was revolutionary. The machine's components were in perfect working order. The physical components inside the young man were not. Deep within, entirely unnoticed, something was going terribly wrong.

In arid climates, the human body dehydrates quickly. Initially, the effect is subtle—producing imperceptible changes long before an individual might feel thirst. Deprived of proper amounts of water, bodily fluids thicken quickly and the heart is forced to work harder to do its job. In a short time, the blood becomes hypercoagulable. As it becomes more prone to clotting, the legs become zones of particular danger. The lower extremities are farther from the churning of the heart, and the veins especially so. By the time the blood has carried its precious cargo to its destination, the initial force that sent it on its long journey is diminished. Robbed of necessary hydration by the desert air, the blood becomes syrupy and sluggish—the veins become breeding grounds for deep vein thrombosis. It's why passengers on intercontinental or other flights of long duration are reminded to get up and stretch their legs from time to time. Sitting up in the same position for great lengths of time increases the probability that blood clots will form in the legs. The young man was in the desert, and he was dehydrated. He slept with his knees balled under his chin in the same cramped quarters where he'd ridden for hour upon hour. Somewhere in the vast network of his lower circulatory system, a bomb was being built.

Eventually, the clot would break free—sent on a return trip to the heart, where it would enter the right atrium. From there, the next stop was the right ventricle, where blood is blasted into the pulmonary artery and into the lungs for oxygenation. Only this time, the blood was carrying a potentially deadly passenger. A large enough clot can cause an obstruction and compromise circulation—a pulmonary embolism. It's not uncommon. The American Heart Association estimates six hundred thousand Americans have one each year. Approximately sixty thousand of those will die.

David Bloom was on top of the mountain. An award-winning journalist, Bloom had risen through the ranks of NBC on the shoulders of his professionalism, tenacity, and creativity. He'd covered major stories from Kosovo to Somalia, hosted major network telecasts, anchored fast-breaking reports from the field, and dissected complicated stories for the American people—putting his heart and soul into doing the best job he possibly could. Ordinarily, such ambition and devotion to achievement comes with a price. Family, personal, or professional relationships often take a backseat—or get ground under the heels of individuals determined to stay on a fast track. Bloom was different. In a business where success often breeds envy and hostility, Bloom was almost universally admired and respected—if not loved outright. Friends, colleagues, and even competitors respected and liked the guy. Associates thought of him as a breath of fresh air: a man who was never too busy or too successful to respond with humility or to share the limelight. And there was practically nothing more important to Bloom than his wife, Melanie, and their three daughters.

For the war in Iraq, Bloom's inventiveness had given birth to what became affectionately known as the "Bloom-mobile." It was a tricked-out, specially adapted version of an Army M-88 tank-retriever—except this contraption was straight from some television engineer's favorite dream. Complete with satellite hookups, computers, long-range microwave radio, and a gyrostabilized camera, Bloom and his colleagues were able to bring the viewing audience images of war previously known only to soldiers themselves. Buzzing through the sands of Iraq with the U.S. Army's Third Infantry Division, David Bloom brought it home. As one contemporary put it, Bloom traded the perks and clothing accounts of a comfy anchor desk to show war from the perspective of a nineteen-year-old infantryman. He wasn't just embedded with the troops; he became one of them: eating MREs, wearing a Kevlar vest over his biochemical protection suit, rakishly grinning beneath his Oakley shades, ducking mortar rounds and RPGs, and sleeping in his cramped and uncomfortable vehicle just as the grunts slept in theirs. It was a quality that had served Bloom well in reporting major stories from O. J. Simpson to Monica Lewinski to Hurricane Andrew.

As one colleague would later say of Bloom, "He wasn't just good on his feet. He was dazzling, and unfailingly human."

Nestled in the middle of nowhere sat Camp Virginia, a curious but orderly and disciplined assortment of military hardware, combat units, tents, mess halls, and reporters. It was just a few days before the first thrust onto the sands of Iraq. Three of my station colleagues—reporter Robert Riggs, photojournalist Billy Sexton, and producer Steve Narisi—were watching something unusual.

Robert, Billy, and Steve had been embedded with the Army's 522nd Missile Battalion out of Fort Bliss. Robert and Billy had followed the unit all the way from

El Paso, Texas, to deployment in Kuwait. Fort Bliss is home to one of the Army's largest air defense artillery units, featuring the Patriot missile system—perhaps the main defense against Saddam Hussein's Scuds and al-Samouds.

Iraqi missiles that couldn't be taken out by Special Forces and air strikes were a danger. Their warheads could be carrying anything from conventional payloads to nerve gas or biological agents. As just about everyone had learned since 9/11, even a single drop of VX or Sarin on the skin was enough to kill a human being in thirty seconds. A cloud of the stuff could wipe out an entire battalion. It was feared Saddam Hussein had far more formidable weapons at his disposal. Every Allied soldier had protective suits and antidote injection kits close at hand. Destroying those weapons meant high technology at every turn, and the people to maintain it. They were soldiers to be sure, but they were twenty-first-century warriors: a cohesive unit that featured people who could disassemble an assault rifle in pitch darkness, get a disabled armored personnel carrier back into the convoy, or figure out the guts of a computerized target acquisition or fire-control system.

So it was somewhat more than surprise and curiosity that Robert and Billy felt when they noticed several members of the 522nd and other units hustling across the sand with what appeared to be plastic sheeting and armloads of bottled water.

In the desert, water is the most precious commodity of all. As Billy would later tell it, "Home was a tent with forty soldiers, chow was an MRE, and showers were few." Deployment anywhere means doing without a lot of things, but the desert means the most deprivation of all—especially when it comes to water. It's more valuable than an armload of diamonds. You can run out of just about anything, and maybe you'll luck out and live, but if you run out of water, you're going to die. Since the first Gulf War, everyone had wised up. The desalinated ocean water supplied by the Saudis was still around, but it tasted like it had been passed through a car radiator. Smart soldiers mixed in packets of Kool-Aid to make it more drinkable. A dash of salt and some extra sugar could turn the Saudi water into a pretty solid energy booster. But bottled water from home—that was the premium. This time around, it was in plentiful supply, but you still didn't waste any of it.

Robert, Billy, and Steve watched for a few minutes as the troops approached a small berm reinforced by sandbags in the middle of the camp, about thirty feet from the front flap of the trio's tent. The troops stretched the plastic tarp across the top and then allowed it to sag in the middle, forming some sort of temporary, shallow basin. It was about two-thirds the length of a man—essentially, a very crude bathtub. More sandbags were placed along the rim on top of the tarp to secure it on all four sides.

And then they started emptying the water bottles into the basin.

A group of soldiers was gathering. Among them were chaplains. As the water lapped up about knee-high in the tub, the point of the effort became clear: They were filling a baptistery.

The three journalists focused on one of the soldiers standing nearby. James Kiehl was a member of the 507th Maintenance Company and was from the small town of Comfort, Texas. As a young man, Kiehl had forged a friendship with a man at his home church, a deacon who had once served in the military. It was an example that Kiehl wanted to follow, although he had not yet publicly committed his life to Jesus. He did that on the eve of battle in the sands of the Kuwaiti desert. Kiehl's new wife, Jill, was back home expecting the couple's first child. Kiehl had decided it was time to put his life aright. He wanted to be baptized—for a lot of reasons, but mainly for his wife and unborn son. It would be a tight fit: The twenty-two-year-old computer repair specialist stood at 6′8″. Kiehl would have to be nearly folded up in order to fit into the cramped, improvised structure—let alone to be entirely submerged in the precious water.

As his comrades and our crew stood witness, Kiehl confessed his belief that Jesus Christ is the Son of God. A chaplain standing with him in the berm placed one hand on James's back, gathered up the soldier's hands in the other, and laid him down into the water. Carefully, he pressed down onto Kiehl's uniformed body until the lanky Texan was completely wet. It was no small task. With an elbow popping up here, and a knee there, it seemed at no point was Kiehl completely immersed at once. But even the most ardent legalist would be loath to nitpick. What mattered was Kiehl's heart, and James Kiehl's heart was completely with the Lord.

And our cameras had caught it all. Within hours, the story had been beamed back to our station. When the networks picked up on it, the "Baptism in the Desert" shot around the world.

From ancient times, it is not unusual to invoke a higher power on the eve of combat: Norsemen prayed to Oden, while the armies of Saladin pledged their lives to Allah and the prophet Mohammed. During the Crusades, Frankish knights were baptized before battle—but always with the right hand extended above the water, so the hand that held the sword could still wield the sword. The soldier's soul could be saved, while his hand was free to sin. Last Rites and blessings have been performed over companies of warriors since Joshua tuned up the trumpets and Constantine turned to Christianity.

On a more practical level, foxhole conversions are as old as war itself, but that scene from Kuwait seemed profoundly genuine. It was right in our living rooms, in almost real time. At the very least, it led to some interesting conversations. Could a believer serve under arms? How could believers justify killing for any reason—and how could a loving God allow it?

However you answer those questions, it is worth noting that Jesus never commanded the many soldiers he encountered to leave the service. What he did command was that they first become his soldiers, willing to obey his commandments, submitting their own pride and willfulness to him—and that was precisely what these gallant warriors seemed to be doing. They were fully prepared to render to Caesar what was Caesar's, if so ordered, but were literally laying down what really counted for God. It caught everyone's attention. Even those of us in television, who have seen much in the way of self-serving behavior or self-protection, were impressed by what we were watching on our studio monitors. Ordinarily, you just didn't see this kind of thing on secular television or the major broadcast networks—and it was all over the place.

But that was not the end of the story.

What happened shortly after that day is still being distilled. The official Army report suggests that on March 23, 2003—because of fatigue, stress, mechanical malfunctions, a horrible chain of avoidable errors, and just plain bad luck—James Kiehl was headed into disaster.

It started three days earlier. U.S. forces were beginning a forty-hour push into enemy territory and the city of Najaf. One commander misunderstood his briefing. Instead of taking Kiehl's convoy around the outskirts of a small town called an-Nasiriyah, the resulting route took them right through the middle of it. In the predawn darkness of the fateful day, elements of the convoy became separated from the main column. They were at the north end of the city before the mistake was finally realized, and a U-turn was ordered. Some vehicles ran out of gas or got stuck in the sand, which opened up huge gaps in the line. Suddenly, the convoy began encountering debris and barricades in the streets, slowing the vehicles down even more. The group had already taken some light small arms fire, but then the entire world seemed to disintegrate at once.

The enemy took advantage of the target of opportunity. Kiehl and his colleagues were engulfed in the intractable "fog of war"—a surreal state of slow-motion confusion in which anything that can go wrong usually does, and almost always at the worst possible time. Iraqi regulars and members of Saddam Hussein's Fedayeen forces furiously hit the Americans as they crossed a bridge, using everything from small arms and heavy automatic weapons to rocket-propelled grenades and tanks. One RPG hit the vehicle carrying Pfc. Jessica Lynch, who was wounded and captured. The firefight lasted for at least an hour before Marines were able to fight their way through and rescue the survivors. Seven Americans were taken prisoner. Eleven soldiers were killed—including James Kiehl.

Kiehl's parents would later say that the pictures of their son's baptism had been a great comfort to them. They had hoped and prayed for that decision for years. As Billy Sexton would tell me later, "That hole dug in the Kuwaiti desert and filled with bottled water is still there in Camp Virginia. I wish the people who casually walk by it daily could know its importance. Sadly, many will never know. For me, I'm reminded daily of God's presence and peace. It's protected me for a long time. I guess it took war to remind me of it."

It often takes war to remind many of us.

Two weeks later, on the morning of April 6th, David Bloom had just gotten off the phone with his wife. As Bloom prepared for another day with the legendary "Marne Division"—as the 3rd Infantry Division is affectionately known—the blood clot deep in his body broke loose and flowed into his chest. The stricken reporter was evacuated to a medical tent, but it was too late.

It fell to a soldier to phone in the first report. "Enemy involvement, none. Civilian. Deceased." David Bloom was thirty-nine years old.

In an email to his wife sent just hours before he died, David Bloom wrote the following words:

> Here I am, supposedly at the peak of professional success, and I could frankly care less. Yes, I'm proud of the good job we've all been doing, but in the scheme of things it matters little compared to my relationship with you, the girls—and Jesus.

We've all heard a lot of debates about what heaven is like. Some people believe there will be gardens and gold, while others expect nothing but a bright bathing light. For myself, I'm not entirely sure. It really doesn't matter. Jesus will be there, and everything else is negotiable.

I imagine that if its inhabitants are aware of anything beyond the borders of heaven, James Kiehl misses his wife and watches the son he never had the chance to meet in life. I wouldn't doubt for a moment that he's made a new friend. I imagine that David Bloom treats him like a younger brother, swapping tales of bedtime stories, skinned knees, and butterfly kisses while they watch their children grow up. They talk of their dreams, their lives, their hopes, their longings—and their deepest, heartfelt prayers to be reunited with their brides and children. God listens in. He joins the conversation. He tells the two men about an energetic youngster in a humble carpenter's shop. He shows them the temple where the young boy amazed the elders, and the river where he stood waist-deep with his cousin. He shows them his bride, the church, and revels in all of her wonderful beauty. Perhaps God parts the clouds and narrows the distance so that these two fellow fathers can look in on their own children—so that they too can *be there*. He shows them the nails that exacted the price, and the blood that paid it. He shows them the empty tomb where it all became possible.

He knows exactly how they feel.

God parted the clouds and closed the distance through his own Son. He became one of us not only to save us, but also to *understand* us. And he longs for us too.

The psalmist wrote, "He knows our frame; he remembers that we are dust" (Ps. 103:14). This is no isolated toy maker who simply wound up the works and then walked away. This is a carpenter who became wood to *completely* understand the furniture—and he never calls us to do anything that he did not do himself. That's the beautiful, pure logic of it.

The Spirit that enabled Jesus of Nazareth to face and endure his own trials and struggles is available to us.

Not too long ago, in the sands of a faraway place, that same power sustained two ordinary men and took them home.

24

Wisdom in the Stillness

Precious Places of Peace

—◦◦◦—

I was the craftsman at his side. I was filled with delight day after day, rejoicing in his presence.

Proverbs 8:30

There are a lot of great places on this earth to get your batteries recharged. One of my favorites is an old steak-house in Chicago. Gene & Georgetti's dates back to an era when a restaurant was a place where people did more than just eat. Situated under the L-track on Franklin Street, it brings you back to the roaring days of backroom deals, strong drinks, and men smoking strong cigars. Not all of that history was pretty, but that's beside the point. When you walk in the door, you're greeted by dark hardwood and a soft amber glow from the lights. The walls bear what seems like hundreds of framed photos containing images of celebrities, regulars, and denizens. The maitre d' looks like he's worked there *since* the forties. Along the bar you'll see finely dressed women and more than a few stout men. On my first visit, they all seemed to be wearing turtleneck sweaters and leather blazers. It was like a scene out of the television show *The Sopranos*. For Gene & Georgetti's waiters, it's their life—and they're a no-nonsense bunch. Whether or not you like the food is purely subjective, but I found my steak to be one of the best I'd ever enjoyed. Of course when my waiter asked me, I wasn't about to tell him otherwise.

A similar place exists closer to my home, although its past might well be more innocent. A Texas woman named Grace Jackson started her little restaurant at about the same time Gene & Georgetti's opened its doors. Jackson's place is called The Ranchman's Café, and it's about as out of the way as you can get. It sits in the little town of Ponder, in the middle of the cross timbers about thirty minutes north of Fort Worth. In spite of the fact that Mrs. Jackson died several years ago, the crowd in her little place frequently exceeds the population of the town itself. Behind the swinging screen door you will find a steak lover's nirvana. There's no concern for cholesterol counts here, and the cuts of meat cover your whole plate. Fries are the standard side order, but you can get a baked potato. The trick is that while you might not need reservations to get a seat, you do have to call ahead to reserve a spud. Country folks like to know you're coming, and they don't like waste. The woman who has made the restaurant's legendary homemade pies for more than thirty years gets to the kitchen at around eight in the morning and drives the three blocks back to her home each afternoon on her motorized scooter. On weekend nights, The Ranchman offers music, and the sound of old tunes played on guitar, fiddle, and bodhran spill through the windows along with the magnificent aromas. Everyone from John Wayne to Warren Beatty and Cindy Crawford to Don Henley has stopped here. Novelist Larry McMurtry saw a church bus through the shutters, and titled a book over lunch—*Lonesome Dove* was once a nearby Baptist church.

When I do stories on places like Gene & Georgetti's or the Ranchman's Café, I answer email requests for driving directions for weeks afterward. But I love it. The idea of sharing such treasures is satisfying.

Then there's Scotland. If God takes naps, that's where he lays his head. Over the course of my career, I've been to a lot of places. Truthfully, I've never found one of those places not beautiful in one way or another. Vibrant cities make one feel awake and alive. Breathtaking landscapes testify to the grandeur of creation. To me, Scotland is the most stunning of all.

Up in the Highlands is Glencoe Pass—one of the world's great natural wonders. Carved by glaciers eons ago, it offers a stunning combination of soaring mountains, gentle flowered meadows, and mysterious glens shrouded by clouds and fog. The road climbs and winds its way through canyons and across cliffs, each mile taking you farther from civilization and deeper into a storybook land of ancient wonder. Since landowners were forcibly removed during Scotland's "Clearances" generations ago, few people live here. Besides the road, a few aged bridges, and the stone walls that have stood here for centuries, there aren't many indications that man has ever been here at all. Some days, the clouds part—frequently with great suddenness—and the soft Scottish weather of the Highlands gives way to rays of sunshine that create a corona of light in the mists of the mountains.

As you round yet another bend in the roadway near a place called Spaen Bridge, you're confronted by a startling sight. During the days of World War II, this is where the British Army trained its commandos. This is where they learned the endurance, teamwork, and initiative to take the fight for the future of civilization directly into the heart of Hitler's Europe. Once the United States joined the war, Americans trained here as well, forming the first brigades of the legendary U.S. Army Rangers. After they were first assembled in Ireland, this was literally their jumping-off place for operations such as the Normandy invasion. Not long ago, I went to this silent and lonely place to film part of a story commemorating the sixtieth anniversary of D-Day. Surrounded by the majestic peaks, unfathomable lochs, and rolling highland meadows, the Commando Memorial stands as a stark testimony to the feats of these relatively few, brave men. Three giant bronze soldiers, their faces set with purpose, stare toward a distant and unseen horizon. Flower bouquets, personal notes, photographs, and even small bottles of fine Scotch whiskey are constantly refreshed at the base of the monument—a perpetual tribute to the long line of soldiers who've fought and died in conflicts from the Falkland Islands to Basra. At the top of the pedestal are three simple words: "Until we conquer." It's one of the most profoundly inspiring places I've ever visited.

If they're man-made, most memorable spots have their creator's name attached. Gene and Georgetti have their names on the sign. Grace Jackson's portrait is reverentially placed inside the Ranchman's Café. Near the base of the Commando Memorial are the etched initials of the artist. But even though he's created some of the most inspirational places you've ever seen, there's no sign or marker anywhere to tell you about J. D. Richmond.

J. D. and I became friends several years ago, and I eventually did a story about him. While you might initially think that there are a lot of people with the same gifts as Richmond, you quickly realize there's no one quite like him anywhere. J. D. is an artist, and his medium is stone—stone fountains, stone walls, and stone panoramas. In fact, J. D. looks like he was chiseled from granite himself. When I met him, he was already seventy-eight years old, but the years of hauling and maneuvering rock had honed his muscles into iron. While not a big man, his hands were the biggest and most powerful I'd ever seen—shaking hands with him was like putting your own mitt into a vise. With a shock of perfect white hair crowning his head, his profile was strong and his eyes bright. The first time I ever saw J. D. he was shuffling along in a beaten-up blue jumpsuit, the same outfit he wore to church on

Sunday mornings. Every pocket was stuffed with wads of paper and notes. A silver spoon was tucked down the back of his collar as a testimony to J. D.'s belief in the healthful properties of the element. A plethora of pens rode on the top of his breast pocket, and he carried an old, well-marked Bible in his hand.

To describe his image as eccentric would be putting it mildly.

I was standing with a mutual friend as J. D. moved by us. My friend said, "There goes a man with a lot of stars in his crown. That guy is a giant." To tell the truth, he didn't look that big. How wrong I was.

I soon came to learn that J. D. was different in every way that a man can be different. Most Christians are satisfied with being regular believers. J. D. wasn't happy with anything less than radical. The first time I introduced myself, he looked me up and down, froze me with an irresistible look, and asked, "Are you transparent?" As I said, eccentric would be putting it mildly.

Before he eventually moved to another city, J. D. and I spent every Saturday morning over breakfast. I began to learn of all the things that he had done. As a child, he'd designed a one-wheeled automobile. As an adult, he'd built dioramas for zoos, vast rock gardens for corporate campuses, quiet fountains for botanical gardens, and more than a few fountains for backyard pools. He'd designed and built an ingenious working geyser for a children's hospital. Few things delighted him more than talking about how he'd stripped to the waist and pulled a sixty-pound pump out of a deep hole with one hand

211

while he was in his seventies. Only one thing delighted J. D. more than finding an unusual stone.

When I finally sat J. D. down for an on-camera interview, he wore his trademark jumpsuit. The fact that he was going to be on television was incidental. He was never changing, never wavering, and always authentic. What you saw was what you got. As he talked, my cameraman began leaning around his viewfinder to listen in. As he paused to change batteries, he asked, "Who *is* this guy?" Frank Lloyd Wright once said every architect must be a prophet. So I answered, "Elijah."

I asked J. D. why there were no markers extolling his work. "Every artist signs his painting," I said. "Why not you?"

J. D. Richmond's answer said it all.

"Well, what I try to do is make it look like I didn't do it. I want it to look like the Lord did it. If I can do that, I've succeeded. I've asked for great glory in my life," J. D. continued, "and got it. But the secret to great glory is great humility."

Humility in the eyes of God isn't a wrestling match to see who can wind up in last place. In reality, it comes from knowing who you *are* in the eyes of God. Most of us tend to dwell on who we are in our own eyes. We measure ourselves by our accomplishments, by our incomes, or by our status. We determine our rank based on how others see us, or how we make ourselves appear to others. But biblical humility literally means to empty ourselves—to abdicate all need for being anything other than what we are made to be. The word Paul uses is *kenosis*—what Jesus did when he surrendered himself to the will of his father (Phil. 2:5–8). It is the secret of his glory. The Word—through and by which everything was made—completely abandoned "self." That's strong stuff.

Self demands credit. We like to see our names in neon and in headlines three inches tall. And yet there's something transcendent about those who do not seek that glory. There's something refreshing about those who just do what they do, and do it simply because they love it. They rarely get rich. They usually don't make headlines. They don't leave fingerprints, autographs, or markers. They're not in it for themselves; as a result, they enrich us. Each leaves an oasis—a place where we can dip ourselves in pure waters and find ourselves recharged by the simplicity of a humble spirit. They are crazy, unexpected, and reassuringly authentic.

I found such an oasis at the foot of a giant monument in a high, remote place that honored men who sought no glory but found it, remembered in the hearts of their families and countrymen for the gift they gave by emptying themselves on the battlefield. And we can find such a place in magnificent stones, stacked to look like the Lord did it.

James, the half brother of Jesus, wrote about living life in the "meekness of wisdom" (James 3:13). He had the privilege to see a life like that up close. Wisdom is never self-serving, and I think that's why on his business card, J. D. Richmond calls himself a "craftsman." During our interview he told me about the eighth chapter of Proverbs, where wisdom is called God's first work of all. When there were no oceans, wisdom was there.

Before God made the fields, wisdom was there. When God measured the foundations of the earth, wisdom was at his side. Wisdom was God's master workman and God's daily delight.

In J. D.'s words, wisdom made God happy. Wisdom made God laugh with joy—I'm sure J. D. does too.

25

Getting the Word Out

Earthen Vessels and Cracked Pots

—⌘—

What does it matter? The important thing is that in
every way, whether from false motives or true, Christ is
preached. And because of this I rejoice.

Philippians 1:18 NIV

How do you react to a rock star thanking God? A lot of
people might hesitate at the thought.

Rock & roll is not usually the first thing that leaps
to mind when one thinks of godliness. Any music can
contain powerful spiritual messages, but the rock song-
book isn't entirely uplifting. There are plenty of songs
and plenty of artists who celebrate or glorify the darker
side of our nature. Even at its best, rock is still a genre

built on our most carnal instincts. In fact, the phrase "rock & roll" itself got its start as a slang expression for sexual intercourse.

But Prince Rogers Nelson took that expression to a whole new level. Most rock fans simply know Nelson as "Prince"—a gifted musician who took a variety of musical styles and combined them into a style that revolutionized the music industry. Beyond his musicianship, Prince is also a consummate showman—and for some, "consummate" might be the operative word. For while Prince's lyrics and melodies challenge convention, his stage shows and persona explore human sexuality in ways going far beyond the merely suggestive. With Prince, sexuality is on full display, accompanied by the pounding rhythms of blues, funk, and rock & roll.

In 2004 Prince was inducted into the Rock & Roll Hall of Fame. First and foremost, he thanked God. He said a few other things too. Most notably, that a true friend and mentor is never someone on your payroll, and that a true friend and mentor is someone who cares as much for your soul as he does for his own. But the first thing he mentioned was God.

How do you feel about that? Given Prince's message and his style of delivering it, was it a contradiction? Hypocrisy? Sacrilege? How about pure blasphemy?

It seems not a day goes by that we don't see or hear an athlete, politician, or actor invoke the name of the Almighty. I see and report stories like that almost every day. Popular perception says most of the people who use God's name frequently don't lead lives that reflect the usage. In fact, many people might say that while

these folks are thanking the heavenly Father, it's doubt-
ful he would be very happy with all they're up to here
on earth.

But a lot of people at the Rock & Roll Hall of Fame that
night—and millions more who watched the induction
ceremony on the cable television channel VH-1—heard
the name of God. It was attached to a thank-you. In
gratitude and praise. As an honor. Prince spoke it out
loud for a whole room of rock & roll rebels and self-
indulgent stars to hear.

Funny how some of us complain that we don't hear
God's name spoken often enough and then turn around
and complain when we hear it spoken at all.

Mel Gibson's *The Passion of the Christ* is one of the
most controversial motion pictures of all time. It was
more like a hurricane than a film. Word of its arrival in
theaters had been filtering out for some time before the
movie actually opened. Fan sites for movie buffs whis-
pered details of what was coming: The movie's dialogue
would be in two dead languages, and the violence and
gore would be extraordinarily realistic. Moreover, most
of the cast members were unknowns, Gibson had spent
millions of his own money to make the film, and no
major distributor would touch it. Advanced screenings
were limited to select audiences, and few if any major
film critics would have a chance to preview it. Reporters
would largely be barred from screenings that did take
place, and those who did attend would be required to
sign documents promising not to publish or broadcast
any reviews. As an air of mystery built around Gibson's
film, so did an army of detractors. Would the film depict

Jews as solely responsible for Jesus's death? Would it give rise to anti-Semitism? As the film approached, the storm around it grew.

And I walked right into the fury. In all honesty, I didn't mean to. A few weeks before the film premiered, I attended a screening at a local church. The next day I wrote an email to a small circle of close church friends. I'd grown up with a very sanitized presentation of Christ's death, but in my heart I could always visualize what the actual event must have been like. Like many other people who've seen *The Passion of the Christ*, it had a powerful impact on me—and I tried to put that impact into words.

These days you can find that note just about anywhere on the Internet. That was my first lesson: In the age of the World Wide Web, there's no such thing as a "small circle" of anything. Each of my friends forwarded what I'd written to their friends. Those friends did the same for their friends. Within a few days, my little note about the movie had migrated a lot farther than I had anticipated. I started getting calls and emails from people all over the United States who'd read it. Within a week, I was getting emails from all over the world: China, the Ukraine, New Zealand, Canada, Russia—everywhere. A man in Europe recently sent me a book containing my little letter! Thirty years of broadcasting, and I might be recognized by a viewer at the grocery store. One little note, and now I was published in France.

Which is not to say I did the right thing. It was just a letter to some friends and not an official "review" for my station. They were just my personal thoughts and not the official position of my company. But like a complete goofball, I'd written that note to my friends on a company computer—and that was a problem.

The company I work for rightfully has stringent standards for all journalists who work under its umbrella. Any reputable and respectable news organization must. Without meaning to, I'd violated those standards. I received a couple of calls from reporters with other organizations who wanted to know how I'd be disciplined, and they were right to ask. I'm sure my superiors got a few inquiries they've never told me about. They held a couple of meetings to establish my motives, but I think the look on my face must have told them: Never would I attempt to say that my beliefs—whether in an email or those expressed in this book—are those of my company in general, or that they are corporate policy. Reporters are entitled to their personal views. We are not entitled to air those views under the auspices of the company banner; even though I hadn't meant to, that's exactly how it came across to more than a few people. I was mortified.

Thankfully, my superiors recognized the difference between an individual exercising intentional disregard and an absentminded dunce. There are a lot of rules in this fast-changing world of mass communication, and with good reason. A hint of bias from a journalist can destroy his or her credibility—and the credibility of his or her organization. As a believer, I represent Christ. As an employee, I represent my employer. It's sometimes a difficult balance. Paul wrote that servants should be obedient to their masters, and that honor and respect

219

should be paid to those to whom it is due. Inadvertently, I'd run the risk of dishonoring my employer. Besides that, the viewer is ultimately my professional master. I'd shown disrespect to those viewers whose beliefs were different from mine. I'd created a stumbling block.

Some people might say that's taking too harsh a view. Some might say that as a believer, I'm obliged to state my beliefs regardless of whether anyone agrees with them or wants to hear them. I disagree, and I think Paul did too. When Paul spoke to the Athenians at the Areopagus, he was *asked* to share his faith—but he still took pains to respect the faiths present in his audience. In fact, he complimented those who held varying beliefs, saying, "Men of Athens, I perceive that in every way you are very religious" (Acts 17:22). Paul understood that the secret to credibility is humility.

Paul would have used his home computer.

I had the privilege of talking to a lot of people of different faiths who weren't entirely pleased with my little missive, and they were almost universally forgiving. I'm grateful for that kind of grace. Moreover, my problems were quickly swept to the back burner by larger controversies, namely, a certain infamous Super Bowl halftime show.

These days, I trundle home and chop out my personal thoughts on my private PC.

Meanwhile, Gibson's movie was setting box-office records. Without a doubt, there will be people who use what they've seen on screen as a license to hate, but that's always been true. Far more people have been touched—millions, in fact. Several polls conducted after the film's release suggest that its message has inclined viewers to see Jesus's death as what it truly was—not a murder, but a willing sacrifice for all. Curiously, some of the film's harshest criticism came not from nonbelievers, but from Christians.

If Prince Rogers Nelson was wrong to have mentioned God at all, Gibson had shouted his name too loudly. One was sacrilegious, while the other was gratuitous. An actor best known for *Braveheart*, *The Road Warrior*, and *Lethal Weapon*, and a man with something less than a sterling past, had made a movie about Jesus? It had to be nothing but opportunistic profiteering, couched in the name of the Almighty. Never mind that Gibson said he had hit bottom and found new relevance in faith, it was all just a good marketing plan. Besides—it was just a *movie*.

One woman wrote me that she could not imagine why Gibson would cast Monica Bellucci, an "unrepentant porn star," as Mary Magdalene. It's true that Bellucci has made several films that appeal to European sensibilities, which are different than those of some Americans. But beyond the fact that the movie may well have been part of Bellucci's own personal spiritual awakening, my response was simple. Traditionally, Mary Magdalene has been portrayed as the woman found in adultery and brought before Jesus. That story seems to have gained its authority from Pope Gregory the Great in the year 591 BC, but if that tradition is based on fact, who *better* to play Magdalene?

Most of the criticism I read, received, or reported on dealt with the graphic violence of the film, usually from

221

people who've never seen someone die violently. The fact is, had Gibson depicted the Passion in its entirety, his movie would have received far more than an "R" rating. It likely could have never been made.

As depicted in the movie, Jesus's flogging was indeed at the hands of the Romans, not the Jews, and Rome had no limit on the number of lashes that could be administered. Many scourging victims died from disembowelment. The Romans also crucified most of their condemned in the nude. The idea of Roman soldiers mocking Jesus's mark of circumcision isn't something our minds easily bear, but it likely was the case. And at the point of death, human bowels evacuate. More than just blood flowed down that cross. His humiliation was complete. I can't think of many people who want to linger long on seeing the King of the Universe that way—but Isaiah did: "He was looked down on and passed over, a man who suffered, who knew pain firsthand. One look at him and people turned away. We looked down on him, thought he was scum" (Isa. 53:3 Message).

To me, there's a simple reason why so many people had a problem with Gibson's gory depiction: If Jesus's ordeal was really that heinous—if his step down from heaven's throne was really that *far*—then sin must really be *that bad*.

No wonder we prefer a decaffeinated Christ. But a PG-Jesus won't get it done.

About five weeks after *The Passion of the Christ* came out, I had another chance to watch the movie with a wonderful group of men and women who lived in a halfway house. The group included recovering addicts, alcoholics, prostitutes, the destitute, and the hopeless. Most had once lived under bridges. Some I'd first met on the streets. Others when they very nearly had a crack pipe still tucked between their lips. Now they'd all handed their lives over to God and were engaged in the torturous process of letting him get them back on their feet. As we sat in the darkened theater, I wondered what their reactions would be. How would they feel after seeing the spilled blood and lacerated flesh? I'd now seen the movie three times, and each time the mostly middle-class audience around me had responded with stunned silence, guilt, and sorrow. Would this group of junkies, hookers, and derelicts feel even guiltier over what *they* had done to put Christ on the cross?

The film ended, and we filed out into the lobby. Imagine my surprise when instead of tears of regret, I saw smiles of joy. They were *happy*. And they were praising God. I was stunned.

I thought about their reaction for a while, and I think I've found the answer for what had happened. Many of the people who've seen *The Passion* are materially blessed. Movie tickets aren't cheap. If you can afford a ticket, you probably have somewhere to live, a nice home, nice clothes, perhaps a nice car or two. Maybe you attend a nice church for the nice lessons. We all like nice things. But Gibson's movie showed something that wasn't nice at all. It showed a scandal, or *skandalon* as Paul called it (Rom. 9:33; 1 Cor. 1:23; Gal. 5:11). And while some of us saw Jesus as we'd never seen him, my friends from the halfway house saw someone they *knew*.

These abandoned, neglected, and abused people saw the King of the Universe abandoned, neglected, and abused. Most had finally been left with only the clothes on their backs, and they saw God with one tunic to his name, stripped in shame. Those who had been mocked and ridiculed saw the Word mocked and ridiculed. Men and women who had been beaten down, spat upon, and humiliated weren't seeing a stained-glass image: They were looking at the Lord of Lords beaten down, spat upon, and humiliated—just as they had been. They didn't just see someone able to save them from themselves and their circumstances. They saw a *brother*.

Instead of feeling guilt, they found hope. But then, the poor, diseased, outcast, and abhorrent have *always* recognized Jesus. People like Dan Leach.

One Sunday morning in early 2004, Leach stood before the Avenue N Church of Christ in Rosenberg, Texas. The twenty-one-year-old told the congregation that he was about to go on a journey that would take him away for a long time and asked for their prayers. Later that day, Leach's father called three church elders to the family's home. His son had a story to tell.

The body of Ashley Wilson had been found less than two months earlier. Wilson's mother had discovered the body in the nineteen-year-old's apartment. Wilson was fully clothed, with a pillowcase over her head, and the cord from her high school graduation gown wrapped around her neck. In a note found nearby, Wilson wrote that she was pregnant, and talked of severe depression. After an autopsy, the local medical examiner ruled the death a suicide. Wilson's parents were never convinced, but the police had nothing else to go on. Then young Dan Leach told his story: It hadn't been a suicide at all.

That Sunday afternoon, March 7, Leach went with his father and the church elders to see the police. Leach had taken great care to make Wilson's death look like a suicide. He had hatched his plan the day Wilson had told Leach that she was pregnant. Leach told the detectives that he had contacted an old friend of the family, a minister, who had advised Leach to admit what he had done. Dan Leach II had strangled Ashley Wilson.

Leach had gotten away with it. The case had been closed. Mystified reporters asked Fort Bend County Sheriff's Detective Mike Kubricht why Leach had confessed. Why had he called the old preacher? Why had he stood before his church? Kubricht told them that Leach had gone to the movies recently and seen *The Passion of the Christ*. "It moved him," Kubricht added. "He felt compelled to come forward with this. He wanted redemption."

A jury will decide Leach's guilt and punishment, but God will judge the young man's heart. No one else is qualified. We do know that the nagging questions of a young woman's family have been answered. As Ashley Wilson's mother told reporters, "If this boy had not come forward, we never would have known."

This was not an isolated incident. A burglar in Southern California turned himself in. A man who'd been on the run from authorities for two years surrendered. A Norwegian neo-Nazi responsible for a string of unsolved bombings walked into a police station and gave himself up.

After watching a *movie*.

It is just a movie. But when I see stories like this, I always think about Jesus sending Peter to fetch a coin from the mouth of a fish. The Galilean fisherman must have thought it was ridiculous, but the money was needed to pay the temple tax, so off he went. As an experienced salt, Peter would have known that only one species of Galilee fish had a mouth large enough to hold a coin. That meant catching a specific kind of fish—a *mousht* in Arabic, or what Italians call a talapia. What were the chances of *that*? I'd love to have seen Peter's expression when he looked in its mouth.

If God can use something as ridiculous as a coin in the mouth of a fish, he can use a movie or rock star.

Paul was right. "What *does* it matter? The important thing is that in *every* way, whether from false motives or true, Christ is preached. And because of this I rejoice" (Phil. 1:18 NIV, emphasis mine).

Striving with God

A Journalist Grapples with Faith and the News

———

I have seen God face to face, and yet my life is preserved.

Genesis 32:30

Jacob was a heel. Literally.

The Hebrew name means one who supplants and undermines. He was a deal maker, but he was anything but honest. A mama's boy who allowed his mother, Rebekah, to coax him into ridiculous intrigue—the scheme to deceive his own father and steal his own brother's birthright. A coward who ran from Esau's anger. Jacob dishonored one wife in favor of another. It took a family feud with his father-in-law to finally get Jacob to face his brother, and even then, he came with a bribe to cool Esau's anger. Jacob was the ultimate game player. Jacob had mostly tried to do what God wanted—but there was a problem. Jacob wanted to do things Jacob's way.

But in his infinite wisdom, God wouldn't give up on Jacob. Somewhere deep inside, Jacob heard God calling. Sometimes, Jacob even answered. Years of wrestling with God finally climaxed one night when the two got together face-to-face. Even with a dislocated hip, Jacob refused to let go, and demanded a blessing. His name was changed to Israel: *"he who strives with God."* Jacob walked differently for the rest of his life, and not just physically.

Thank God that *God* doesn't let go.

I have forgotten so many stories over the years. On my desk sits a bundle of amazing stories from the past few weeks. Thumbing through them, I'm awestruck. Here's one from Arkansas about a man who recently awakened from nearly twenty years in a coma. His wife remained faithful to him all those years, and his infant daughter is now nineteen years old. Terry Wallis says he will walk again—for her.

Here's another story about a young man who was riding along in his Jeep when he had an accident. The force of the collision ejected him from the vehicle, and he might have been killed—except for the fact that the collision threw him high enough that strands of power lines above the street caught him in the air. Instead of being electrocuted, the wires saved his life—and rescue workers were able to get him down safely.

And here's the story of outdoorsman Aron Ralston, who was trapped by a falling boulder on the side of a cliff in southwestern Utah. Alone, out of water, and running out of time, Ralston used a pocketknife to amputate his right arm and free himself from the stone that held him in a death grip—before hiking out of the canyon on his own. The story instantly caught international attention, especially for those people who recalled Jesus's advice to "amputate" those things that threaten us. If there's ever been a more vivid testimony toward the truth of that logic, I haven't heard of it.

I wish I could call to mind all the past illustrations of Jesus's presence in circumstances that seemed to defy anything holy that I've witnessed. I have seen faint hints of his goodness in the midst of evil and tragedy many times, but I have a confession to make.

For most of my life, those examples didn't penetrate very far into my heart.

For most of the thirty years I've been in broadcasting, I've had the privilege to do charity work, support good causes, speak before civic organizations, and do a few things behind the scenes that might have made some small difference. I was proud of those moments and have always been extremely humbled by the great people I've had the chance to meet. That, especially, has been the best part of my career.

But none of it really made an impression. Not down deep.

Whenever I had the chance to spend time with some sick children, or do something nice for someone, it was as if the meaning of the experience never really sank in.

Maybe it made a huge difference in someone else's day or life, but it never truly changed me. I did what I did because it seemed right, or because it was good to give back—and sometimes, simply because I liked the way it made me look. Community involvement is great for a broadcaster's resume. It was more than that for me, but not much more.

Whenever there was some terrible story in the news, I was more given to react in disgust than to look for the cross. Many times, the news only served to harden my heart or provide a nice setup for a good punch line. The personal tragedies of others became fodder for gallows humor, or a joke at some politician or religious leader's expense. Abraham Lincoln once said, "I laugh because I must not cry." I took that as license to laugh at everything, instead of looking closely for meaning. It was all a matter of how I saw things, instead of how they looked through the eyes of Jesus. What I'd done—what we all do—was to put myself on the throne reserved for God.

I knew all the Sunday school stories from my youth, and even responded to them as a young boy. I preached. I spoke in youth groups and at devotionals. I took theology in college and even thought about becoming a preacher. Through it all and up until now, the things I've witnessed in life confirm there is a God, but his real message to me rolled right off. As in the parable, the seed fell on hard ground and never took root. Then finally, one day God got through.

There comes a moment in every person's life when our ground is broken and the events of life plow our soil.

Only then are we ready to receive God's meaning. Only then can it take root and grow. After more than forty-two years, God brought out the plow for me. It wasn't that he hadn't been trying, but my farmland had become parched and arid. Dramatic measures were needed to rehabilitate the land. God delivered a miracle. He taught me that the job Jacob and I both wanted was already taken.

God taught me that I needed to get off his throne.

The Bible talks about people who have it almost right but still leave out the fundamental element. Everything we see or do is useless unless it is totally viewed through this one, single lens—even in the worst or most impossible of circumstances. Paul wrote about it in 1 Corinthians 13. Many of us know that chapter by heart. It says something very personal to me. As a broadcaster, it hits home.

I might be very eloquent, a terrific writer, convince you to trust me, say the things you like to hear, say all the *right* things, and even have a huge audience, but if I don't have love, I'm nothing more than a cheap, annoying noisemaker. I might be able to entertain, inform, analyze, and provide insight. I might even be able to get things done for people and change things for the better—but if I don't have love, I am nothing. I can do all the charity dinners and banquets in the world, make appearances all over town, do great things for good causes, and work so hard that I eventually keel over. A lot of people might even come to the funeral and say some very nice things about the things I did, but if I don't do it for the right reason—the gut-level, real, only-one-that-matters reason—I have gained not one single thing. It's all about love.

Love waits. It's kind. It doesn't take advantage and it doesn't brag. It isn't puffed up and it isn't in your face. Love doesn't want, and it doesn't get hurt when it doesn't get what it wants. It never rejoices over people's problems or lies, but it's ecstatic over those things that are good and right. Love can bear up when everything else fails. It believes all things, hopes all the time, and can endure anything.

I'm paraphrasing what Paul wrote of course, but that's essentially it. He goes on to say that everything we put much stock in will eventually go away. All of it. But that kind of love—the kind of perfect love that casts out fear—authors something else. It makes the "perfect" visible. Not just later, when the imperfect passes away—but *now*. I believe that getting closer to that kind of love means we become able to see more clearly in this life, and not just later. When we get closer to that kind of love, we begin to understand fully. The closer we get to the cross, the better we are able to see it. What's more, we are called to look for it. It's the open door and the unique opportunity. It's visible in a lifetime of chances to really live. It's the light that banishes despair and brings illumination to the darkness. Sometimes, we get so used to seeing only darkness with our eyes that we forget that the vast majority of what we call "light" exists outside of the visible spectrum. But the light is there.

Anywhere. Everywhere. Even in the news.

Especially in the news.

This is not to suggest that I've got a handle on all this. Far from it. What I've written here are merely my takes on God's incontrovertible truths—and only he is the final arbiter. Arrogance, cynicism, pride, and discouragement are demons I still battle with every minute of every day. The desire to be the world's centerpiece and the filter through which all things are judged is with me even now. That war is constant. But thanks to God, I don't have to fight alone. He shows me the cross in ways I could never see on my own. My favorite verse in the entire Bible remains Jeremiah 33:3. The Revised Standard Version reads, "Call to me and I will answer you, and will tell you great and hidden things which you have not known." Good journalists have good sources, ask good questions, and keep an open mind: I've finally got my notepad and pencil out, and I'm taking notes.

My employer and my viewer still expect an unbiased, balanced reporting of the facts. It's not my job to color a story with my own personal beliefs, and I won't. I don't have to, and that's the good news. God will be revealed, regardless. He *will* be glorified, no matter what. His kingdom will prevail. But what do we do when everything around us simply becomes too much to handle?

When lepers, outcasts, and the poor were brought before Jesus, he didn't turn away because the sight was too depressing: He dove right into the middle of them. When the Samaritan spotted a bruised and battered man by the side of the road, he didn't walk on because the sight was too hard to bear: He took pity and took action. Creation was filled with bad and terrible things even two thousand years ago, but Christ's commandment is more than a call to prayer for a hurting world. Perhaps no one understood this better than Jesus's own half brother, James. In his letter, James writes like a man who didn't come to see his sibling for who Jesus is until much later—like a man convicted and called to action by his own previous lack of acceptance. Nowhere is that more evident than in James 2:14–17. Eugene Peterson's marvelous translation, *The Message*, conveys the principle best:

> Dear friends, do you think you'll get anywhere in this if you learn the right words but never do anything? Does merely talking about faith indicate that a person really has it? For instance, if you come upon an old friend dressed in rags and half-starved and say, 'Good morning, friend! Be clothed in Christ! Be filled with the Holy Spirit!' and walk off without providing so much as a coat or a cup of soup—where does that get you? Isn't it obvious that God-talk without God-acts is outrageous nonsense?

But it goes far beyond a call to action regarding the individuals we see. Jesus's call goes to the very basics of how we look at all things.

We worry. We fret. We're scared. We want to pull down the curtains, close the blinds, tuck our head under the pillow, and pull the covers over us, hoping we can escape. We hear of wars and rumors of wars. Nation rises against nation. There are earthquakes, famines, terrors, and great signs from heaven. Good people are delivered up to evil kings. Entire industries are built on prophecies of doom and destruction. Even well-meaning believers fall victim to the trap of predicting the end of it all, and every discouraging story in the news seems to reinforce the foreboding of impending catastrophe. From a sixteen-year-old smoking grass to the convulsions of nations, everything seems to testify that all is lost—and yet, see what Jesus says: "When these things begin to take place, look up and raise your heads, because *your redemption is drawing near*" (Luke 21:28, emphasis mine).

Jesus sees opportunity. Christ sees deliverance. The news is a call to prayer, action—and hope. Behind it all is the cross.

It's there to see. All we have to do is quit fighting it and look.

Jody Dean has won an Emmy, twice won the Dallas Press Club's "Katie Award," and has been the recipient of several other awards during his thirty-year career in television and radio. He currently works at a major network affiliate in Dallas-Fort Worth. Dean attended Abilene Christian University and is a lifelong resident of Fort Worth, Texas.